IMPRESSIONIST INTERIORS

IMPRESSIONIST INTERIORS

Published on the occasion of the exhibition

IMPRESSIONIST INTERIORS

at the National Gallery of Ireland, Dublin
10 May – 10 August 2008

Distributed by the National Gallery of Ireland
Copyright ©2008 National Gallery of Ireland and the authors

ISBN 978-1-904288-30-5

Catalogue Editor: Janet McLean
Copy Editor: Brendan Rooney

Catalogue Design: Jason Ellams
Printed in Dublin by: Colorman (Ireland) Limited

Cover image:
Federico Zandomeneghi, *A Letto* (*In Bed*) (detail), 1878 (cat. 26)

Details:
Paul Gauguin, *The Painter's Home, rue Carcel*, 1881 (p. 3, cat. 19)
Edouard Manet, *Interior at Arcachon*, 1871 (p. 14, cat. 22)
Edgar Degas, *Sulking*, c.1870 (p. 30, cat. 12)
Edgar Degas, *The Song Rehearsal*, 1872-73 (p. 52, cat. 18)

This publication was produced with the financial assistance
of the Department of Arts, Sport and Tourism.

THE DEPARTMENT OF
ARTS, SPORT AND TOURISM

Supported by

6

Director's Foreword

7

Sponsor's Foreword

8

Acknowledgements

9

Lenders to the Exhibition

11

Janet McLean

Impressionist Interiors: An Introduction

14

Hollis Clayson

Threshold space: Parisian modernism betwixt and between (1869 to 1891)

30

Suzanne Singletary

Le Chez-Soi: Men 'At Home' in Impressionist Interiors

52

Catalogue

Janet McLean

146

Selected Bibliography

Director's foreword

Over a period of just less than one hundred years France passed from being a monarchy to an empire to being a republic. At the heart of this transformation was Paris, which by the mid nineteenth century had become the pre-eminent cultural centre for the visual arts in Europe.

The revolution which most impacted the fine arts was Impressionism, an approach to painting which broke with the academic traditions of the past, elevating the loosely painted canvas, spattered with brilliant brush strokes – for the most part, to the status of a finished work of art.

But it wasn't only in the realm of the physical act of painting that the Impressionists broke new ground, but also in their choice of subject and how they chose to present it. In the latter half of the century Paris had become a sprawling, industrial metropolis, where the traditional order was being usurped, replaced by a growing bourgeoisie with disposable income and time to enjoy it. Gone was the mad maze of streets of the medieval city – replaced by Haussmann's cavernous boulevards. Gone was the gloom of night, banished by gas and electricity. Gone was the old social order following the trauma of the Revolution, the Franco Prussian War and the Paris Commune of 1871.

The selection of paintings which constitute this wonderful display of works by the Impressionist masters and their contemporaries beguile the eye and intrigue the mind. Outwardly the images contain all the attractive attributes which make the art of the age such a popular phenomenon; images of a lifestyle to which we can still relate painted by gifted artists in a style which appeals to modern sensibilities. Best known for their landscapes, the compositions which make up this show concentrate on the private and public spaces where people communed or sought solace in retreat.

The essays and commentaries included in this publication enrich our understanding of the works presented for display, providing insights into aspects of the lives of the artists and their contemporaries, which reflect the excitement at the heart of Baudelaire's *Le peintre de la vie moderne*.

The National Gallery of Ireland is greatly indebted to the lenders, both institutional and private, who generously have agreed to contribute to this unique exhibition. Thanks are also due to KPMG who have assisted with the funding for the show and the European Commission Representation in Ireland for sponsoring the opening reception on 9th May Europe Day.

Finally a special word of gratitude is due to Janet McLean, Curator of European Art 1850-1950, who devised and curated 'Impressionist Interiors'.

Raymond Keaveney
Director
National Gallery of Ireland

Sponsor's foreword

When the first works of the Impressionists came to public attention in nineteenth-century Paris, they not only broke the established rules of academic painting but often met with a hostile response from many of the critics. Since then however, the enduring popularity of the Impressionists has been well established the world over.

Thus it is to the great credit of the National Gallery of Ireland that we have this unique opportunity to view *Impressionist Interiors* this summer. The National Gallery is an outstanding asset to our capital city and to Ireland as a whole and it is testament to the standing of the Gallery that so many wonderful and well known paintings have been secured for this exhibition. Works by Manet, Monet, Renoir, Degas and others are sure to enthral a wide range of Irish and overseas visitors in the months ahead.

In keeping with our commitment to the arts, KPMG is genuinely proud to play a role in supporting such an exciting project and to help make this exhibition possible. Whether you have a life long love of art or are just starting to explore the area, we hope that you enjoy your visit to *Impressionist Interiors*.

Terence O'Rourke
Managing Partner
KPMG

Acknowledgements

This exhibition and catalogue have been made possible through the support of colleagues within the National Gallery of Ireland and the expertise and goodwill of numerous individuals and institutions both nationally and internationally.

I am sincerely grateful to the private lenders and the custodians of public collections who have so generously allowed their important works of art to be included in this exhibition. The following people have been especially gracious in their assistance - Guillaume Ambroise, Graham W.J. Beal, Stéphanie de Brabander, Caroline Campbell, Christopher Brown, James Carder, Guy Cogeval, Tim Craven, Barbara Dawson, Anne-Birgitte Fonsmark, Dickon Hall, Gry Hedin, Laurence Le Cieux, Jay Levenson, Katharine Lochnan, Pat Murphy, Lynn Orr, Sylvie Patry, Sylvie Ramond, Joseph J. Rishel, Séverine Seba, Guillermo Solana, Sidsel Maris Søndergaard, Paul Spencer-Longhurst, Charles K. Steiner, Matthew Stephenson, Anne Sumner, Linda Thomas, Suzanne F. Wells, Timothy Wilson and Barnaby Wright. Many thanks are also due to His Excellency Yvon Roé d'Albert, French Ambassador to Ireland, to Isabelle Etienne and Elisabetta Sabbatini. I am hugely grateful to Alan Hobart for his support and enthusiasm. I would like to add a special acknowledgement to the late Philip Conisbee, who was among the first to offer help and who gave his vote of confidence to the project with unreserved kindness.

While the advice and expertise of many individuals helped to shape the exhibition, particular thanks are due to Anne Anderson, John House, Philip McEvansoneya and Annette Wickham. Hollis Clayson and Suzanne Singletary deserve special mention for engaging wholeheartedly with the concept of *Impressionist Interiors* and for their insightful contributions to the catalogue. Jason Ellams who did a wonderful job designing the catalogue was patient, encouraging and a pleasure to work with.

The organisation of *Impressionist Interiors* has been an exceptional collaborative undertaking. I am grateful to Raymond Keaveney, Director of the National Gallery of Ireland, for his steadfast support and assistance in securing loans. I am especially appreciative to Fionnuala Croke, whose door was always open and who ensured that every question found an answer. The professionalism of Marie Bourke, Síle Boylan, Valerie Keogh, Louise Morgan, Orla O'Brien, Susan O'Connor and Kim Smit ensured the smooth running of the show. Thanks are also due to Sergio Benedetti, Leah Benson, Sighle Breathnach-Lynch, Barry Carroll, Ranson Davey, Sheila Dooley, Joanne Drum, Lydia Furlong, Roy Hewson, Anne Hodge, Enda Hogan, Kevin Kelly, Adrian LeHarivel, Camille Lynch, Donal Maguire, Pat McBride, Marie McFeely, Niamh MacNally, Helen Monaghan, Andrew Moore, Luke O'Callaghan, Chris O'Toole, Emma Pearson, Catherine Sheridan, Felicia Tan, Adriaan Waiboer and to Muirne Lydon and Colm Short. A special thank you to Brendan Rooney on whose friendship and expertise I have relied heavily.

I am especially grateful to my family for their support and encouragement and in particular would like to thank my daughter Róisín, who has shared her first seventeen months with this project, and my husband Tom Farrelly for *everything*.

Janet McLean

Lenders to the exhibition

Denmark

Ny Carlsberg Glyptotek, Copenhagen: cat. 33

Ordrupgaard, Copenhagen: cats. 24, 25

France

Musée d'Evreux: cat. 13

Musée des Beaux Arts de Lyon: cats. 4, 40

Musée Marmottan Monet, Paris: cat. 23

Musée d'Orsay, Paris: cat. 9

Pau, Musée des Beaux-Arts: cats. 10, 11

Germany

Staatliche Museen zu Berlin, Nationalgalerie: cat. 14

Italy

Galleria d'Arte Moderna, Palazzo Pitti, Florence: cat. 26

Collezione Mondadori, Museo Civico Palazzo Te, Mantova, Italy: cat. 27

Norway

The National Museum of Art, Architecture and Design Oslo: cat. 19

Spain

Carmen Thyssen-Bornemisza Collection on loan to the Museo Thyssen-Bornemisza: cat. 28, 45

United Kingdom

Ashmolean Museum, Oxford: cat. 41

Barber Institute of Fine Arts, University of Birmingham: cat. 42

Leeds Museums and Galleries: cat. 35

Private Collection, Courtesy of Pyms Gallery, London: cats. 2, 3, 5, 31

Scottish National Gallery of Modern Art, Edinburgh: cat. 37

Southampton City Art Gallery: cat. 39

Tate: cat. 30

United States

Detroit Institute of Arts: cat. 1

Flint Institute of Arts, Flint, Michigan: cat. 20

The J. Paul Getty Museum, Los Angeles: cat. 29

House Collection, Dumbarton Oaks, Washington, DC: cat. 18

The Metropolitan Museum of Art, New York: cat. 12

Museum of Fine Arts, Boston: cat. 8

The Museum of Modern Art, New York: cat. 38

National Gallery of Art, Washington: cats. 17, 21

Philadelphia Museum of Art: cat. 34

Saint Louis Art Museum: cat. 43

Sterling and Francine Clark Art Institute, Williamstown, Massachusetts: cat. 22

Wadsworth Atheneum Museum of Art, Hartford, CT: cat. 15

Janet McLean

Impressionist Interiors: An Introduction

Writing in defence of Edouard Manet and the Impressionists in 1876, Stéphane Mallarmé commented 'Why is it needful to represent the open air of gardens, shore or street when it must be owned that the chief part of modern existence is passed within doors?'[1]

Today, as in 1876, the art of the Impressionists is primarily associated with the open air - with sunrises, landscapes, boating parties and *dejeuners sur l'herbe*. In the late 1860s Claude Monet, Auguste Renoir, Frederic Bazille and Alfred Sisley became fascinated with the effects of natural light upon colour and composition. Following the lead of Courbet, Corot and artists of the Barbizon School, they extricated themselves from the restrictive enclosures of the atelier and ventured outside to paint *en plein air* in the environs of Paris and in the forest of Fontainebleau. Their gravitation towards the outdoors was largely accelerated by new developments in pre-mixed paints. The availability of the metal paint tube liberated artists from grinding and mixing powdered pigments, it made their equipment more portable and provided an unprecedented intensity and immediacy of colour. These practical developments found expression in a painting style that was correspondingly looser, brighter and breezier, in essence *Impressionist*.

Despite this zeal for painting outdoors, it cannot be denied that in the 1870s and 1880s, as Mallarmé observed, 'the chief part of modern existence' was 'passed within doors'. Artists associated with Impressionism did not just aspire to be painters of light and air but aimed to be modern artists and thereby painters of modern life. Exhibitors at the eight Impressionist exhibitions held between 1874 and 1886, eschewed the staged historical re-enactments, the fancy-dressed classicism and the imagined Orient sanctioned by the official Salon. Rejecting traditional Academic conventions of representation these artists set out to paint what they experienced and shared a common motive to present scenes from contemporary life with a random immediacy.

In 1876 the writer Edmond Duranty published *La nouvelle peinture* (*The new painting*). This thirty-eight page pamphlet coincided with the second Impressionist exhibition and insightfully outlined the novel realism that Duranty perceived in the work of the artists who exhibited at the Durand-Ruel Gallery that year. Although no artists were specified by name, it is clear that Duranty saw Edgar Degas as the leading light in this exciting modern movement. He observed that these 'new painters' had emerged from the sky-lit spaces of the garret studio 'back among men, out into the real world'. Their choices of subject matter exemplified the fact that 'our lives take place in rooms and in streets, and rooms and streets have their own special laws of light and visual language.'[2] For Duranty the modern city and the apartment interior were intrinsically connected to the art of those who practised 'The new painting'.

The city of Paris is essential to the concept of the Impressionist interior. It was there, for the most part, that the 'new painters' or Impressionists lived, trained, sold their art and socialised. Although developments in the railway system enabled them to enjoy access to the suburbs, the coast and the countryside, artists such as Edgar Degas, Berthe Morisot, Paul Gauguin and Mary Cassatt were, in the main, city dwellers. During the 1860s Paris was radically transformed by Baron Haussmann under the directive of Napoleon III. His intensive programme of urban renewal resulted in grand boulevards cutting clear arteries through the city, the introduction of artificial light sources, the infiltration of natural light through public squares and gardens and the development of modern apartment living. By the 1870s cafés, theatres and café-concerts took on a new lease of life. Rapidly they became common arenas where social boundaries could be crossed and conventions broken and where men and women, working classes and bourgeoisie, had the potential to intermingle or at least to gain a new awareness of each others existence. Both Degas and Edouard Manet navigated these new urban interiors with perspicacity and found a wealth of subject matter in the Opéra house, cafés and bars that had become homes from home for many Parisians.

For Impressionist artists, informal domestic subjects proved powerful antidotes to the lofty historical set-pieces endorsed by the Academy and official Salon. Furthermore as the modern city was being celebrated in art and literature, the idea of the home was simultaneously being idealised as a private retreat removed from the anonymity of the urban throng. Edmond Duranty seemed almost relieved when he stated 'at last the subject matter of art includes the simple intimacies of everyday life in its repertoire'.[3] The artists who painted scenes based around domestic interiors typically showed friends and family members in informal poses, relaxing on sofas, daydreaming in bed, bathing, reading and eating.

In the latter half of the nineteenth century the middle-class interior took on new symbolic significance. The collection and display of ornamental objects within the home became a way of indicating the occupant's taste, knowledge, interests and past experiences. Looking once more to Degas, Duranty stated that painters of modern life should remember to depict their figures in context and not against neutral backdrops. On the same account, he said 'the language of the empty apartment must be clear enough to enable us to deduce the character and the habits of its occupant.'[4] Zacharie Astruc's *Parisian Interior* (1874, cat. 13) and Gauguin's *The Painter's Home rue Carcel* (1881, cat.19) exhibited at the first and seventh Impressionist exhibitions, are very different pictures in terms of style, technique and composition. Yet the strategic display of decorative objects in the interiors they depict reveals in similar ways how the inhabited interior could signal individuality, or perform as a manifestation of the 'self'.

The majority of Impressionist artists came from comfortable bourgeois or petit-bourgeois backgrounds. For the urban middle-classes, the workplace (like the place of leisure or entertainment) had become noticeably separate from the home. In 1876 Degas and Gustave Caillebotte were somewhat unusual in exhibiting modern-life interiors depicting men at work. Degas's *Portraits in a Cotton Office (New Orleans)* (1873, cat. 10) and Caillebotte's *The Floor Scrapers* (1875, Musée d'Orsay, Paris) presented the contrasting working worlds of the businessman and the artisan. Caillebotte went on to paint scenes set within bourgeois apartment interiors but for Degas, the workplace interior continued to be a significant source of inspiration and a favoured context for his modern-life subjects. In many of his paintings, including *Sulking* (c.1870, cat. 12), the boundary between the workplace and the domestic interior is intriguingly unclear.

Although Impressionist artists were affiliated by close friendships and shared artistic interests, it must be remembered that they did not work to a manifesto or from a single viewpoint. Instead the 'group' was made up of a loose collective of individuals for whom painting from direct observation was a unifying principle. Whereas Degas was resolutely an artist of interiors and human interactions, Alfred Sisley was by contrast, an artist of the outdoors.

While this exhibition focuses on the concept of *Impressionist Interiors*, it cannot be denied that the experience of painting *en plein air* was an overwhelming priority for artists such as Monet, Morisot, Renoir and Camille Pissarro. In this respect it is not surprising that windows, balconies and threshold spaces play a prominent role in Impressionist paintings of the interior. Locating their compositions by such apertures and openings enabled artists to paint in natural light and to colour their interiors accordingly. It also, quite cleverly, gave Impressionist artists opportunities to paint 'paintings within paintings' and they would effectively use windows to frame a landscape, seascape or sky viewed from indoors. Windows allowed them to exteriorise the interior space. As Duranty eloquently stated:

> From indoors we communicate with the outside world through windows. A window is yet
> another frame that is continually with us during the time we spend at home, and that time is
> considerable. Depending whether we are near or far, seated or standing, the window frames
> the scene outside in the most unexpected and changeable ways, providing us with constantly
> changing impromptu views that are the great delights of life.[5]

Impressionist Interiors brings together a group of paintings and drawings which reveal some of the many and varied ways in which Impressionists and artists within their circle, engaged with interior spaces – public and private, domestic and social, realist and symbolist, everyday and holiday.

1 Stéphane Mallarmé, 'The Impressionists and Edouard Manet',
Reprinted in Moffett et al 1986, p. 30.
2 Duranty quoted in Moffett et al 1986, p. 44.
3 Duranty quoted in Moffett et al 1986, p. 45.
4 Duranty quoted in Moffett et al 1986, p. 45.
5 Duranty quoted in Moffett et al 1986, p. 45.

Hollis Clayson

Threshold space: Parisian modernism betwixt and between (1869 to 1891)

Authors of proto-Impressionist and Impressionist art of the Parisian everyday, adventuresome
Parisian modernist painters and *peintres-graveurs* alike, gravitated to the *mise-en-scène* of the
metropolitan interior, and used it to explore the sheer difficulty of making sense of modern urban
experience. Indeed the investment in the interior is among the thematic hallmarks of nineteenth-
century art.[1] The interior acquired multiple valences and meanings: understood primarily as
domestic space, it was also an image of domesticity, and the locus of the inner world of the self.[2]
The frequent recourse to the interior in art instanced its manifold modernities – this was *the* era of
the interior[3] – and recognised its power to serve as a social and psychological laboratory.

The architectural consequences of and evidence for the skyrocketing centrality of the interior and
the epoch's signature exaltation of domesticity were sizable. Donald J. Olsen has shown that insofar
as the two dominant institutions and focuses of loyalty in Paris during the second half of the 1800s
were the family and the nation-state, 'the nature, size, external appearance, internal arrangement,
and location of the family dwelling occupied a central place in urban theory and practice.'[4] Sharon
Marcus explains the imbrication of interior space and private feeling. From the 1850s and 1860s,
she writes, 'the 'interior' no longer marked a space whose physical difference from the exterior was
neutral, obvious, and thus trivial; it became identified with *le foyer*, the family home and hearth'.[5]

Christoph Asendorf's headline-style declaration is unequivocal: 'The nineteenth century is the
century of the interior'.[6] As is Walter Benjamin's formulation: 'The de-realised individual creates a
place for himself in the private home.'[7] In other words, in the 1800s, domesticity and home-centred
private life were more central, but also more worried over than hitherto. While the interior was
understood as a haven in a heartless world (for men), or a kind of sheltered nest that compensated
for the loss of connection to nature caused by industrialisation (for men *and* women),[8] per Charles
Rice the interior as a cultural form always bears its 'newly illuminated impossibility as a space of
retreat and immersion.'[9] While at the same time, the porosity of the dwelling and its susceptibility
to invasion by the world outside were also understood as threats to its serenity and further
characteristics of modernity.[10]

Threshold space, the spatial *ne plus ultra* of permeability, had special purchase on thinking the
interior because it was literally 'on edge' – both unclear and a site of inherent tension because of
its composite identity. Just as interior rooms inhabited by elites were becoming more and more
specialised and clearly defined, the threshold did not conform; it did not unequivocally belong

to one room or one private or social function or another. When a drawing or sitting room, for example, gave onto a balcony, it was neither fully inside nor outside. And when a space fell between a social and a private use, it belonged exclusively neither to the family nor to visitors.[11] It was threshold space in which the strain intrinsic to various moments and sites of modernity, including the new domesticity sequestered in the interior, could be 'seen' and examined. Quoting Victoria Rosner: 'a way of life built around separation and specialisation encounters difficulty when faced with transitional or in-between states that resist categorisation. Such states are architecturally embodied in the threshold, the space that forms a bridge between two discrete rooms.'[12]

Thus the threshold, a superlative theatre of everyday private life in the Parisian modernist imagination, was tailor-made to anchor scenarios of modernity at its most concentrated, exemplary, and fraught. The art works discussed here utilise diverse composite, transitional, intermediate, and hybrid locales – both inside and out of doors – in which to stage examinations of Parisian life: the balcony, windowed drawing room, indoor/outdoor cabaret, and the omnibus. Understanding art works of this kind as investigations of contemporary life conducted in the often perplexing and stressful conditions of modernity (mostly metropolitan and mostly private), the present account, while not denying personal investments, will part company with readings of the Impressionist 'interior' that identify art works thus located, especially if within the artist's very own home, as exclusively self-documentation and autobiographical.[13]

i. Solitary women hemmed in

Four extraordinary canvases (figs. 1 – 4) represent contemplative, solitary women located at (or near) the border between the drawing room and the 'world beyond,' instanced by a window or balcony.[14] The drawing room (or parlour) worked well as a locus of solitude, but it was a social area in the apartment or house, used to welcome visitors, and also often coded 'feminine.'[15] Each painting construes its setting as an exemplary space of femininity, but emphatically not as a downgraded periphery of modern life and its modernities, but as its second centre. The four art works articulate urban space and experience as realms of privacy and seclusion. The celebrated other centre of modern life was the so-called masculine metropolis;[16] a public realm based on mobility, consumption, and display, whose representations are barely evoked in this essay.

Berthe Morisot's *The Artist's Sister at a Window* (1869, fig. 1, cat. 21), exhibited in the Salon of 1870, represents Edma Pontillon née Morisot, Berthe Morisot's sister, close friend, and painting partner for the previous twelve years. When Edma Morisot married Adolphe Pontillon on 8 March 1869, she moved to Lorient and stopped painting.[17] What had been a collective painting practice became a solitary one: Berthe Morisot's alone. While this rupture is a personal condition of the canvas, it is

not, strictly speaking, what the painting is about. As Anne Higonnet writes: 'Morisot treats family members and strangers alike. The democracy of fashion levels distinctions. If we did not know from later titles and biographical information that the figure in a white *déshabillé* seated by a window was Morisot's sister Edma … how else would we know?'[18]

What counts is the picture's arresting definition of a visibly absorbed and somewhat stressed woman on the brink, both spatially and psychologically. The key dynamic in the picture is the conflict between the sister's determined focus upon her fan and 'the world outside' that ostentatiously beckons beyond the apartment balcony. She has pulled her chair up to be close to the opened French windows and the opening's access to the buildings beyond, but she wears 'at home' clothing and her attention is focused determinedly downwards instead. Moreover the plenitude of the interiority of the woman in white is indexed by the attention she pays to a mere marker object, a purely aesthetic distraction, her fan. Her focus upon the patch of bright green on the fan almost seems visually to inoculate her against the charm of the greater expanse of the same green paint used to describe the awnings on the facing building. Quoting Higonnet again: 'Behind Morisot's women's reserve we sense a life all the more intense because it is withheld.'[19] The painting thus stages a fascinating quarrel between the lure of the brightly-hued world of the street, on the one hand, and the threshold woman's access to it but simultaneous disregard for it, on the other. This careful positioning on the brink endows the young woman with an undeniable gravitas and hints at her self-actualisation through day-dreaming.

Claude Monet's *Meditation: Madame Monet Sitting on a Sofa* (c.1871, fig. 2) is another formidable threshold picture, which makes compelling use of the topos of the seated woman betwixt and

between inside and outside. This is apparently the only painting Monet executed while in London, where he journeyed to escape conscription during the War of 1870, that he exhibited while there.[20] It was unusual vis-à-vis Monet's interiors with figures from the 1860s continuing into the 1870s in its use of a shallow, enclosed space, and the profile placement of the model, Camille Doncieux.[21] While her book and the painting's original French title (*Méditation*) might imply a scenario of self-sufficient indoor female musing, what actually triggers the painting's 'action' and not inconsiderable tension is the electricity of the connection between Camille's actively pensive, slightly up-turned face and the intensity of the bright stripe of curtain barely shielding the glow of the outside world at far right. It deserves to be read allegorically as a rumination upon exile from conflict; as a female allegory of longing for the volatile outside world, which, though immediately adjacent, is inaccessible to this pensive seated woman. In a more general sense, that is, considered apart from the artist's biography, the canvas examines a paradigmatically modern subject: a contemporary young woman's contestation of the conditions of containment prescribed for women in circumstances of the new domesticity – in which home could be experienced by women as a 'consistently interiorised and even carceral space'.[22]

Pierre-Auguste Renoir's *Portrait of Rapha Maître* (1871, fig. 3), was also made in a circumstance of retreat, albeit of a different order, from France's Terrible Year. He painted it in Paris in the spring of 1871 (the date 'avril 71' adjoins the signature) following his seven-month absence from the city. It was thus painted during the Paris Commune and shortly after Renoir's demobilisation – he did army service near Bordeaux during the Franco-Prussian war – and brief follow-up stay in the Hautes Pyrenées with one of his officers.[23] The large, florid, and intensively floral standing portrait was his first painting that year, and the most accomplished art work he would make during 1871. It would be difficult not to read it as part of an attempt on Renoir's part to block out the rising tide of conflict in April in the quarter of the city, the faubourg Saint-Germain, where he apparently found work space during the Commune.[24] It is also, of course, a threshold picture. Therein resides both its force and

fig. 4. **Mary Cassatt (1844-1926)**
Young Girl at a Window, 1883-1885
Oil on canvas, 100.3 x 64.7 cm
Corcoran Gallery of Art, Washington, DC

singular difference from (and superiority to) the run-of-the-mill 'fashionable modern bourgeoise on display in the sitting room' picture which it only superficially resembles.[25]

Renoir's portrait of the common-law wife of his old friend Edmond Maître, a young Belgian woman (last name unknown but 'Mme. Edmond Maitre to the concierge'), defines the extravagantly clad young woman – the lace and silk outfit is up to date fashion – as the proverbial bird in a gilded cage. The almost preposterously ornamented room (pots and pots of blooming spring flowers, a cage containing four birds, floral trellised wallpaper, a richly textured textile covering the bird cage) houses the standing Rapha Maître in an imprisoning or at least claustrophobic embrace, and her facial expression initiates a narrative of regret, disappointment, and longing for elsewhere albeit of an intensely introspective cast. Unlike the typical Alfred Stevens scenario, Renoir's subject is both facially grave and her glance aims at the space beyond the cage of birds. Her face underscores the immensity of the separation between a cosseted woman of the parlour and the streets and boulevards outside, but she also marks allegorically the weight of the gulf between those hiding from

the Commune and the April 1871 street-fighting between the insurrectionary Communards and federal army troops. Renoir's superb invention of a gilded woman ever so gingerly contesting her restriction to a hyper-ornamented private space – even her glance down at her fan registers a measure of despondency and resignation – and the allegorical sub-current that stirs within it emboldens us to disagree with Colin Bailey's ascription to it of an attitude of nostalgia: 'Renoir's *Rapha Maître* cannot be said to reflect this social dislocation in any obvious way, but painted at a time of extreme uncertainty…its celebration of fashionable domesticity might be interpreted as nostalgic at least'.[26] We insist here instead upon the portrait's circumstantial contingency.

Mary Cassatt also intensified the ostensible interior lives of her sitters and enhanced the fascination of her art works by giving her models access to while refusing the panoramic prospects enabled by a perch upon a threshold. As Judith

Barter has usefully observed about *Young Girl at a Window* (c.1883, fig. 4), and other works by Cassatt: '[Her] women are drawn to the light, but reject the view'.[27] Pointedly (perhaps too pointedly) looking down rather than up and across at the buildings and trees, she disregards the view from what is probably the artist's own apartment balcony.[28] The discrepancies between space and behaviour, and between the setting and the pose, do not end there. Though impeccably turned out and ready for an outing in elbow-length gloves, white day dress and matching stylish hat – she is emotionally frozen in a state of focus-free inexpressivity, and physically trapped in a wedge of space bracketed oddly by the hidden household to the right and the city beyond the black iron railing. The clash between her easy access to an unobstructed urban view and her failure to avail herself of it contrasts sharply with the keen visual curiosity of the dog (the artist's dog), shown to have no such scruples. The restrained mien and body of Cassatt's sitter appear to document an instance of the successful confinement of women within the domesticity-saturated *foyer*.

ii. *Yearning at the window*

Gustave Caillebotte's *Young Man at the Window* (1875, fig. 5), among the painter's exhibits in his first 'Impressionist exhibition' in 1876, broached for the first time in his work the theme and *mise-en-scène* of looking out the window at the city of Paris.[29] Gustave's brother René posed on the second floor of the family apartment at the corner of rue de Miromesnil and rue de Lisbonne in a fashionable bourgeois quarter of the Right Bank.[30] This threshold protagonist, who unhesitatingly commands the open window, contrasts strongly with the women we have discussed above, poised reticently or frozen on the brink. Caillebotte's observer, seen from behind, forthrightly addresses the view beyond the open glazed doors and stone balustrade assuming a paradigmatically forceful masculine pose: his firmly-planted, widely-spaced legs exude somatic and emotional command and control. His body appears to convey authority and ease, which successfully breaks through the barrier separating inside from outside. With the effectiveness of an electrified fence, this same invisible wall kept the women discussed in part i, cautious female occupants of threshold position, from possession of the outdoors.

That said, a contrary reading of the man looking out the window is more persuasive. Along these lines, authors of the 1994 Caillebotte exhibition catalogue have observed: 'These openings [of Caillebotte's windows onto streets, rooftops, or courtyards] provide views of what is, in effect, another interior: that of the city'.[31] This statement helps to characterise the hemmed-in quality of the man at the window; the ways in which his commanding manly posture addresses and controls nothing but a cave-like expanse of almost deserted stone and metal. The tiny woman in profile walking through the centre of his field of vision is a meagre catch indeed in the wide net cast by his unimpeded even impertinently poised body. The ostensible restlessness that propelled him from his nearby chair to the open window resembles the condition of a sequestered invalid more than that of an empowered and unconstrained *flâneur*.[32] Indeed this Parisian man looking for something out the window – his body registers determination not dreaminess – is the perfect thwarted *flâneur*. Or perhaps 'thwarted *flâneur*' is an oxymoron by the 1870s. Following the indispensable formulation of Priscilla Parkhurst Ferguson, Caillebotte's man at the window would be read instead as a highly legible image of the consummate *flâneur* of his day – a figure of alienation and detachment, of being in the city without being of it.[33] Placing a man like this in threshold position generates a probing assessment of urban masculine ambition face to face with its limits and discontents.

Caillebotte's slightly later canvas, *Interior: Woman at the Window* (1880, fig. 6), functions as a virtual pendant to the *Young Man at the Window*. In this canvas, which features another powerless figure at a Parisian window, the gender reversals and expansion of a cast of one to several *dramatis personae* are the key moves to note.[34] A male domestic partner ostentatiously engages the newspaper providing a plot thread of spousal inattention with the resultant hurt and frustration driving the woman to the window. How extraordinary, however, that the painting has been taken merely to thematise 'conjugal

boredom',[35] rather than a more capacious view of a vexed female response to her containment within a contemporary, shared urban apartment interior. Like the man in *Young Man at the Window*, this painting's protagonist is on deck at the threshold and also seen from behind, but she faces closed windows covered and filtered by 'the muslin of inner curtains'.[36] Her visual purview is thus extremely limited: only the cognate floor of a twin facing building, bearing the gold letters of advertising, constitutes her view. Indeed, the flash point of the painting's *mise-en-scène* is the inquisitive female subject's evident concentration upon the exposed triangle of a neighbour's curtained apartment window, directly below the alphabetic avatar of commercial culture. But the particularities of predictable gender characteristics do not stop there: she is restless and longs (like a man), but as a woman she is also nosy. As we follow her gaze which fixes upon the rhyming curtains directly across, we realise that she is engaged in spying; in looking in upon an equivalent, inquisitive female prisoner of the interior directly across the way.

iii. In company in between

Édouard Manet's *Interior at Arcachon* (1871, fig. 7, cat. 22), depicts his wife, Suzanne Leenhoff Manet, and Léon Koella Leenhoff, her son (in company the boy was referred to as her brother; he was perhaps Édouard Manet's son or the son of his father, Auguste).[37] In Manet's painting, Suzanne and Léon relax dreamily in the light-filled front room of the rented 1860s seaside chalet where the painter joined his family to recuperate from exhaustion and illness; they had already been sent south out of harm's way during his war service in the capital.[38] The rental near Bordeaux also offered shelter from the (eventual) Paris Commune.[39] Their one-month stay began on the 1 March; the Commune was declared on the 18 March. We confront a canvas therefore that inscribes an ostensible double repose, that of its sitters mirroring that of its war-weary author.

At first scrutiny, the painting indeed impresses most onlookers as a low-key record of serene, daytime familial intimacy within a rented drawing room as stress-free space. The open, glazed terrace doors mediate between the inside and nature beyond, and display a stack of segments of the beach, the bay, a tiny *pinasse* (distinctive local boat), the dunes, and sky above. The commanding, accessible rectangular

fig. 8. **Mary Cassatt (1844-1926)**
Scène d'intérieur (*The Visitor*), c.1880
Soft-ground etching, aquatint, etching, drypoint, plate,
plate: 39.69 x 31.12 cm, sheet: 52.07 x 39.69 cm
National Gallery of Art, Washington, Rosenwald Collection

field of nature at the exact centre of the upper half of the canvas makes this particular interior into a threshold space. The expansive view of sky and water helps the space occupied by the mother - nineteen-year-old son duo to breathe by supplementing and aerating the indoor zone that contains their proximity. A scrupulous examination of the small painting's subtle choreography and design reveals the canvas to be an unexpectedly complex threshold picture.

Léon, in sun-limned, near profile, glances up temporarily from his books. He chews on a pen as he woolgathers. His angle of view and folded up compact body signal his resistance or indifference to the lure of the sea. The line of sight created by Suzanne's oblique gaze seaward (while she takes a break from her writing) runs counter to that of her son. The crisscrossing vectors of their visual interest, combined with the compositionally imposing third 'figure' in the room (the large brown wooden table *mise en valeur* before and by the azure bay outside), create a complex circuitry of connection and separation, attention and inattention, within the intimacy of a reunited family trio living out an unusual kind of vacation.

While the quietude of their coexistence cannot be gainsaid, Manet went to some pains to divide them and to carve the space into 'his' and 'her' zones. Her side is ornamented (fireplace, gilt-framed mirror, a clock, patterned rug, cushy chair, foot rest), while his is comparatively Spartan (simple wooden chair, pattern-free wallpaper, barren wood floor). The manifold contrasts do not add up to the insinuation of conflict, but rather connote stasis or disengagement. The comparative liveliness of the imposing table that divides them deserves a word.[40] The liveliness of its paint handling (along its vertical core and around its lively feet) endows it with an animated presence that approaches the uncanny. Its animation far outstrips the restrained liveliness of the two humans adjoining the imposing table in the same space. The piece of furniture thus both contrasts to their absorptive interiority and lack of connection, and constitutes an opaque wall between them. It works very effectively to drive a proverbial wedge between two family members sharing a parlour threshold space during a moment of repose.

Mary Cassatt's print, *Scène d'intérieur* (*The Visitor*) (c.1880, fig. 8), speaks to anxieties about, even threats triggered by, the penetration of the interior by outsiders.[41] Apropos of the sense of unease that permeates the work, Judith Barter is right to observe: 'While Cassatt's interiors are microcosms of urbane Paris, as well as the loci of familial bonding, social exchange, quiet reflection, and solitary activity, they can also feel suffocating'.[42] *Scène d'intérieur* stages an awkward encounter between the (seated) rightful occupant of the room and the extremely stiff and ill at ease standing visitor, whose mottled body seems uncannily transparent thanks to Cassatt's expert use of aquatint on her garment. The glow of daylight through the panel of translucent figured curtain (*contrejour* lighting) silhouettes the discomfited and slightly grimacing caller, and endows the claustrophobic drawing room with threshold potential if not its full realisation. The silhouetted guest's refusal of the outside – she faces away from the window – echoes the strained indifference of the contained woman on the balcony that we scrutinised in Cassatt's *Young Girl at a Window*. The subtle lighting conditions in the print – the darkness of the two figures against the bright white patches of window light – help guarantee that the get-together between the two women appears shadowy in substance as well as appearance.

While nothing more complicated than the visitor's acceptance of an invitation to draw her chair closer to her hostess may be described here, Cassatt nonetheless maximises its complexity and suggestiveness by her picturing of the event. The visitor's grip on the chair is surprising, indeed eye-catching, because it is off kilter and eccentric (why grasp its back all the way over to the opposite side?). The peculiar hand and arm position combines with the visitor's apprehensive, albeit simplified, facial expression,[43] to hint that the outsider has imported unease through the door. In this nuanced etching, Cassatt pictures a cornerstone of bourgeois social life, the welcoming of a visitor into that oxymoronic world of a private space for social encounters, through the self-conscious lens of belief in the fraught quality not just of the modern interior, but of encounters between American hosts and French guests in the sequestered spaces of the female domestic sphere.[44] The patterned scaffolding created by the forms of the chair back, combined with the visiting woman's arm and sharply-defined body contours, creates a visually striking spidery grid and an effective marker of intersubjective and spatial tension.

iv Hybrid space out of doors
Edgar Degas's lithograph, *Mlle Bécat at the Café des Ambassadeurs* (1877-78, fig. 9), set in an extremely complex indoor-outdoor nightclub (*café concert*) space, relies upon industrialised light as a sign of technological urban modernity, but also of venality and gaudiness in the big city via the juxtaposition of new-fangled light fixtures and a tawdry performing woman. Quoting Sue Welsh Reed and Barbara Stern Shapiro: '[The lithograph] exhibits every form of natural and artificial lighting that could manifest itself in a nocturnal scene: a large gas lamppost, a cluster of gas globes, and a string of lights, seen at the right, are reflected, along with a prominent hanging chandelier, in the mirror

at left behind the performer. In the dark sky, the moon shines through the trees of the Champs-Elysées, while fireworks send down streamers of light. Even a small patch of light is glimpsed in the orchestra pit. Moreover, Degas's characteristic use of reflected footlights is clearly implied in the figure of the singer, who is brightly lit from below.'[45] The bewildering array of lighting forms, coexisting and competing in this intricate black and white image, conducts the viewer across the boundary between indoor and outdoor light fixtures and functions, and thus between interior and outdoor space. The print's mongrel illumination helps emphatically to define this corner of the Café des Ambassadeurs as a threshold space.

The date of the print falls within a particularly volatile era in the ongoing history of the industrialisation of light in Paris.[46] Textual evidence of Degas's familiarity with intricate technical details of these innovations in his own back yard is demonstrated by the post script he added to an 1879 letter to Félix Bracquemond about plans for the next Impressionist exhibition: 'The Company Jablockof proposes to do the lighting with electric light'.[47] But the decisive proof of the artist's knowledge and use of up to date urban lighting gear is in the work itself.

Mlle Bécat inhabits the stage of the Café des Ambassadeurs among the trees of the Champs-Elysées. The fluted columns of its proscenium are noticeable along with the outdoor audience area's signature lamps that lit the garden beyond. Emélie Bécat is represented here at the beginning of her period of fame singing her signature, absurd ditty about the love between two sea creatures, a shrimp and a turbot, which she performed at the Ambassadeurs from 1875 to 1885.[48] The complex assortment of white lights that we have already inventoried enhances the theatrical bravado of the singer's hallmark performance gesture. The intricacy of the visual patterning is striking, but so is the synergy (the mutually inflecting dialogue) between the impropriety of the performer's angular motions and the tawdriness of so much light. And despite the constant reference to 'gas globes' in the art historical scholarship on these art works, it is right to wonder if Degas might not have been referencing instead the simultaneous (and no doubt dazzling, jarring, and vulgarising) presence of two lighting systems – gas plus electricity – on the same premises.

The French art historian, Bruno Foucart, threw down the gauntlet in 1985. 'Consider that we are almost incapable of saying if the light in certain of the greatest impressionist tableaux is that of gas or already of electricity'.[49] Lines from Guy de Maupassant's short story, 'Claire de Lune' (1883), archived by Walter Benjamin, nudge us towards the identification of the globes in Degas's lithograph as electric ones: 'I reached the Champs-Elysées, where the cafés concerts seemed like blazing hearths among the leaves. The chestnut trees, brushed with yellow light, had the look of painted objects, the look of phosphorescent trees. And the electric globes – like shimmering, pale moons, like moon eggs fallen from the sky, like monstrous, living pearls – dimmed, with their nacreous glow, mysterious and regal, the flaring jets of gas, of ugly, dirty gas, and the garlands of coloured glass.'[50] Louise Lipincott and Andreas Blühm tempt us down the same taxonomic path: 'Modern artists attempted to render the new lights, attracted by both the night life and the visual effects they engendered. Manet, Degas, and Toulouse-Lautrec painted the eerily-lit bars and brothels, often exaggerating the odd colour spectra of gas or electricity.'[51]

The eye-numbing dazzle of the light, but also the abstract design possibilities presented by the pure white circles of the club's 'moon eggs,' to crib from Maupassant, obviously engaged Degas. The consequent complexity of the visual rhyming and dialogue he builds between light fixture and female entertainer–each a sign of modish brashness positioned to reflect and play off one another– is the main aesthetic event in the clockwork lithograph.

Mlle Bécat performs on a stage backed by the glitzy reflective surface of a mirror, long associated with the ornamentation of the interior, but the singer addresses top-hatted audience members and musicians (at right are the necks of two double basses) 'out there' – in a zone that connects to the inside space of the column-bordered stage, but she simultaneously connects with an outdoor space into which fireworks can safely descend. This spatial hybridism, combined with the baffling boundary-crossing combination of lighting forms, secures the identity of Mlle Bécat's world as an exemplary border zone.

Griselda Pollock's assessment of Mary Cassatt's colour etching, *In the Omnibus* (1890-91, fig. 10), provides an excellent foundation for considering its bus interior as a threshold space: 'Cassatt's print is not an interior scene, but even outside the home, women occupied the spaces of the bourgeois family, which, of course, was always permeated by 'an outside' in the person of servants'.[52] The central event in the print is indeed the contrast between the inattentiveness of the stylish 'natural' mother and the (paid) childminder's solicitousness of the elegantly dressed child on her lap. In this episode of public transportation taken through Paris across the Seine (seen through the three planar omnibus windows), the class dynamics that enable a cosseted bourgeois family life at home are exported to and displayed in public. The modification that Cassatt undertook between a preliminary

fig. 10. **Mary Cassatt (1844-1926)**
In the Omnibus, c.1891
Soft ground etching, drypoint and colour aquatint,
plate: 36.5 x 26.8 cm, sheet: 43.4 x 29.6 cm
Museum of Fine Arts, Boston, Gift of William Emerson and
The Hayden Collection - Charles Henry Hayden Fund

drawing and etching the plate for the colour print – she deleted a bourgeois man in the tram (seated next to but, like the child, ignored by Madame) – underscores the artist's interest in making social difference qua legible hierarchy between employer and servant the centre-piece of this particular study of a corner of contemporary city life. Though as one of ten colour prints made and shown as an ensemble in 1891 at the Galeries Durand-Ruel, one takes Barter's point about the change: 'This deletion, as well as the total absence of men in the final series, indicates that the artist wished it to represent the hours of a woman's day'.[53]

What further characterises the colour print is its figuration of a double uprooting. The domestic scene of child care is deracinated from home, and the inquiring bourgeois woman – whose oblique glance instances her desire for engagement with the city both geographically and temporally 'beyond the tram' – is cut off from the metropolis proper while confined to the bus with the child and servant. That Cassatt staged a 'cutting off' or severing of the *bourgeoise* from 'the world' within a tram resonates with Wolfgang Schivelbusch's discussion of the distinctive loss of self and sensory control associated at the time with the new modes of viewing the world through a window during rides in another form of contemporary urban mass transit, the railway passenger train.[54]

This representation of a moment and space suspended between home front and outdoors in the French capital might also deserve discussion in light of Cassatt's own assertions of transnationality – a betwixt and between position in the register of nationality – very recently rebuffed and denied by close French artist colleagues (when she was shut out from exhibiting in 1891 with the *Société des Peintres-Graveurs*).[55] Which is to say that the thematisation of rootlessness and sequestration in an explicitly liminal urban space, a threshold between the more clearly demarcated spheres and spaces of city life, may be both a trenchant comment upon modernity and the artist's own thwarted cosmopolitanism in conditions of ascendant French xenophobia at the fin de siècle.

* * *

This essay has examined ten Parisian modernist genre pictures set in threshold space, the liminal zone par excellence, made by seven allied artists. Its principal goal has been to call attention to the strong affinity that these 'Impressionist' artists conceived between some of the defining forms of modernity (especially as experienced by women) and in-between spaces that resist categorisation. In the later nineteenth-century modernist imagination, then, the private individual's drawing room was indeed her box in the world theatre, when and if she summoned the temerity to breach the barrier and enjoy the play.[56]

Acknowledgments. I offer my heartfelt thanks to Janet McLean for inviting me, quite out of the blue, to write this essay. Holles Houghton, Jacob Lewis, Andrew Nogal, Peter Parshall, Mary Dailey Pattee, David Van Zanten and Jason Vrooman also deserve my gratitude.

1 Michael Fried (following Edmond Duranty) argues that interiority and its 'absorptive worlds or cloisters' defined the thematic or spatial modernity of much nineteenth-century French painting. Fried 1996, pp. 259-61.

2 Silverman 1988, p. 25.

3 Rice 2007.

4 Olsen 1986, p. 89.

5 Marcus 1999, p. 148.

6 Asendorf 1993, p. 119.

7 Benjamin 1978, p. 155.

8 Asendorf 1993, p. 125.

9 Rice 2007, p. 35.

10 Walter Benjamin could again be invoked: 'the intoxicated interpenetration of street and residence….comes about in the Paris of the nineteenth century'. Benjamin 1999, p. 423.

11 'Apartment interiors were laid out in accordance with a rational scheme that for many years enjoyed almost universal acceptance. Every apartment had public areas for show, private areas for intimate family gatherings, and purely functional spaces.' Roger-Henri Guerrand, 'Private Spaces,' in Perrot 1990, pp. 366-67.

12 Rosner 2005, pp. 61-62.

13 See, for example, Todd 2005, p. 7.

14 In Paris, the years covered by this essay could also be called the Era of the Balcony. See Loyer 1988, pp. 139, 251 and 354.

15 Rosner 2005, p. 64. See also Juliet Kinchin, 'Interiors: nineteenth-century essays on the 'masculine' and the 'feminine room'' in Kirkham 1996, pp. 12-29.

16 Pollock 1988, pp. 50-90.

17 While the setting resembles a Parisian milieu, it is possible that the canvas was painted in Lorient where Berthe Morisot visited from June through early August. Anne Schirrmeister, 'La Dernière Mode: Berthe Morisot and Costume,' *Perspectives on Morisot*, in Edelstein 1990, p. 110.

18 Higonnet 1992, pp. 113-14.

19 Higonnet 1992, p. 116.

20 House 1978, pp. 636-39, 641-42. See also McConkey 1995, pp. 15-16, 160-61 and Chu 2005, pp. 45-48.

21 House 1978, p. 642.

22 Marcus 1999, p. 152.

23 Bailey et al 1997, pp. 114, 116, 275-76.

24 See House 1978, p. 199 and Bailey et al 1997, p. 114.

25 Such as Alfred Stevens, *The Duchess* (formerly known as *The Blue Dress*), 1860s.

26 Bailey et al 1997, p. 114.

27 Barter 1998, p. 66. A perfect foil to this painting by Cassatt is Édouard Vuillard's *Marie at the Balcony Railing* (1893). See Cogeval 2003, p. 146, no. 88.

28 Barter 1998, note 55, p. 102.

29 Distel et al 1994, p. 148.

30 Distel et al 1994, p. 148.

31 Distel et al 1994, p. 143.

32 In this spirit, Rodolphe Rapetti writes, 'The man's posture (he is the painter's younger brother René), hands in his pockets, apparently staring at a female silhouette in the street, the armchair facing the window, the deserted city, the motionless carriage – all speak of idleness, of time wasted'. Distel et al 1994, p. 142.

33 Ferguson 1994, pp. 80-114.

34 A later treatment of the same theme is Paul Signac's *Sunday* (1888-90). For the painting and its studies, see Ferretti-Bacquillon et al 2001, pp. 149-55.

35 Distel et al 1994, p. 158.

36 Huysmans 1883, quoted in Distel et al 1994, p. 158.

37 Nancy Locke proposes that Léon's father was Manet *père*. Locke 2001.

38 Clayson 2002, pp. 208-33.

39 Wilson-Bareau and Degener 2003, pp. 76-77.

40 Its jauntiness looks forward to a better-known, also highly-animated table in a slightly later vanguard canvas: the red table at the left in Paul Cézanne's *Une moderne Olympia* (1872-73).

41 For further discussion see Clayson (forthcoming) and Pollock 1998, p. 160.

42 Barter 1998, p. 66.

43 The visitor's face is even more anxious and pinched in the related drawing for *'Interior Scene'* (c.1881, Cleveland Museum of Art). See Barter 1998, no. 43, p. 264.

44 I have elsewhere tried to argue that Cassatt's domestic themes explicitly engage and explore the tensions of Franco American social encounters. See Clayson 2001.

45 Reed and Shapiro 1984, catalogue no. 31, p. 94. See also Boorsch 2000, p. 48.

46 See Schivelbusch 1988.

47 Kendall 2004, p. 84.

48 Shapiro 1980, pp. 153-64.

49 See Foucart 1985, p. 148.

50 Benjamin 1999, p. 570.

51 Bluhm and Lippincott 2000, p. 35.

52 Pollock 1998, pp. 169 and 172.

53 Barter, p. 84. The drawing is reproduced on the same page.

54 Schivelbusch 2004, pp. 92-93.

55 On the exclusion, see Mathews and Shapiro 1989, pp. 45 and 68. My mention of trans-nationality in connection with this print references Mary Dailey Pattee, 'Crossing Boundaries: An Analysis of Trans-nationality in Mary Cassatt's *In the Omnibus* (1891)', for Williams College Graduate Program in the History of Art, 14 December 2005.

56 This is a mischievous paraphrase of 'His drawing room is a box in the world theatre', Benjamin 1978, p. 154.

Suzanne Singletary

Le Chez-Soi: Men 'At Home' in Impressionist Interiors

Visitors to the second Impressionist exhibition of 1876 found amid the sun-filled, highly saturated landscapes of Claude Monet, Auguste Renoir, Berthe Morisot and Camille Pissarro, several dimly lit, insulated bourgeois interiors contributed by Gustave Caillebotte. These contracted spaces—corners of rooms in his family's Paris apartment—telescope the viewer behind the building's opaque facade and showcase men, mainly the artist's relatives, as the most visible occupants of these sequestered spaces. Their activities are mundane and unremarkable; they eat lunch, stare out of the window, play the piano. Through highly contrived spatial strategies, Caillebotte thrusts the viewer into these rooms, constructing an immersive environment and effecting a fusion of subject and object—as well as artist and viewer—that destabilises the division between objectively rendered architecture and subjectively experienced space.[1] Equally compelling is Caillebotte's concentration on a modern theme intrinsic to the Impressionist project, namely middle-class men 'at home'.

In his 1846 essay 'On the Heroism of Modern Life', poet-critic Charles Baudelaire challenged artists to abandon the Academic practice of history painting and to embrace modernity, an appeal he reiterated in *The Painter of Modern Life* (1863).[2] In addition to population growth, redesign and expansion under Napoleon III and urban planner Baron Haussmann, and revolutions within the social and political spheres, Paris by mid-century had seen the industrialisation of labour and its removal from its habitual setting within the worker's dwelling. This decisive shift transformed the identity of the house and resulted in a fundamental split between public and private spaces. Concurrently, the tasks performed in specific rooms within the house changed as communal living and working areas were replaced by more private, individualised domains. As early as the 1830s, the English word *home* had migrated into the French language and signified an isolated, self-contained domesticity. Its wholesale appropriation, rather than translation, and common usage by the French bourgeoisie underscored their recognition that the house had undergone a radical redefinition.[3] As artists moved from the studio to the streets and suburbs to chronicle 'modern history', the house increasingly emblematised a personal sanctuary, a refuge ideologically removed from the turmoil and instability of civic arenas. Key corollaries to the public spaces of the urban milieu—perused and re-presented by the Baudelairean *flâneur*—were the private spaces of *home*, considered redolent of femininity, and the locus of flights of fantasy, personal longings and elusive memories. Images of the modern domestic interior served as potent pendants to Impressionist scenes of the city. No less vital than landscapes or urban vistas were close-range, intimate views of figures who would have been enveloped and homogenised within the anonymous crowd, but who assume full agency as protagonists of private life, a social and phenomenological construct with particular resonance during the nineteenth century.[4]

The valorisation of the house as an essential site of modernity surfaced repeatedly in avant-garde criticism, notably in Edmond Duranty's pamphlet, *La nouvelle peinture* (1876), a commentary on the Impressionist's second group show at Durand-Ruel galleries. Duranty championed the domestic interior as a modern subject on a par with the streets, advocating '…the observation of the intimacy of man with his apartment', and accorded particularised meaning to objects in rooms—'furniture, fireplaces, curtains, and walls'—that exude a personal character in synchrony with the room's inhabitants.[5] Like Émile Zola who defined Impressionist painting as a 'corner of the world seen through a temperament',[6] Duranty underscored the subjectivity at the heart of modernity. *The New Painting* sanctioned the invention of a visual language analogous to 'the special laws of light and expression' found in 'rooms and streets' that propels the viewer both physically and psychically into the space to absorb the embodied and imaginative experience of the artist.[7] As early as the Salon of 1859 Baudelaire famously hailed imagination as the 'Queen of Faculties', endorsing a subjectively determined vision of modernity.[8] In his manifesto poem, 'Correspondances', from *Les Fleurs du Mal* (1857), Baudelaire outlined the *modus operandi* by which physical and psychic processes intertwine, elucidating the permeability that links external stimuli with internal experience. For the poet, sights, smells and sounds emanating from objects and places trigger associations embedded in memory that move the artist, and vicariously the viewer, to imaginative, interior spaces.[9] Throughout *Les Fleurs du Mal* and *Le Spleen de Paris*, domestic spaces function as persistent foils to Baudelaire's urban vistas. For example, in the prose poem, 'One o'clock in the morning' ('A une heure du matin'), the house is portrayed as a refuge for the inveterate *flâneur,* a place where the '…turn of the key will…for the moment, separate me from the world', elsewhere described as the 'Horrible City!' The poet's room offers sustenance and restoration, its objects and spaces animated by 'souls of those whom I have loved, souls of those whom I have sung'. Only within the enclosed parameters of the familiar can the 'silence and solitude of the night' be tapped 'to produce a few beautiful verses', the poet's only hope for spiritual redemption.[10] Writing of Baudelaire and nineteenth-century Paris in *The Arcades Project* (1930s), Walter Benjamin proposed that interiority as a psychic state became synonymous with modernity and functioned as a by-product of a moment in history when 'the phantasmagoria of the interior' provided the lens through which all perception was filtered. Benjamin positioned the interior as the linchpin of modernity and anchor for the private individual.[11] Emphasis upon the domestic arena as a central component of contemporary experience, and a fundamental ingredient of the 'modern life' touted by Baudelaire, rendered the house and its occupants as cutting-edge subjects pursued by male and female artists alike. *L'espace privée* was posited as the 'backstage' to the 'onstage' of the urban spectacle, a place where private emotions can be enacted.[12] In the words of Duranty, at home 'the individual will be at a piano…He will be having lunch with his family or sitting in his armchair near his worktable, absorbed in thought…When at rest, he will not be merely pausing or striking a meaningless pose before the photographer's lens. This moment will be a part of his life as are his actions'.[13]

The gendering of space through the delineation of 'separate spheres' emerged quite early in the century, with the public sector of city and commerce designated 'male', countered by the 'female' zone of hearth and home.[14] This reductive formulation masked the dynamic interchange that existed between interior and exterior, in which the parameters of one informed and shaped the exigencies of the other.[15] Bourgeois men, for example, freely occupied both realms and, unlike middle-class women, moved at will between public and private arenas. Moreover, something of the social nature of Haussmann's grand boulevards and *places* spilled into the new *appartements*, though in highly controlled circumstances. César Daly, architecture critic and author of the nine-volume *L'Architecture privée au XIXe siècle sous Napoleon III* (1864-77), prescribed the ideal, rationalised apartment as functionally configured, with the most accessible, reception spaces of *le foyer* and *le grand salon* contrasted with the cloistered rooms reserved exclusively for family, including bedrooms and study. For Daly 'this double aspect… naturally indicates a primary division in the dwelling place. For public life…one needs the largest and richest rooms of the residence. For family life, one needs the interior apartment, with its character of intimacy and comfort'.[16] Family quarters were secluded and protected, the inner sanctum in a sequence of progressively more hermetic chambers. Only in these rooms could inhabitants enjoy a freedom and introspection impossible within the constraints of bourgeois rituals and public personas, constituting an oasis for world-weary men.

The subject of men 'at home' assumed a particular valence during the Second Empire (1852-70), subsumed within renewed cultural focus upon proprietary masculinity. During the conservative reign of Napoleon III and the early years of the Third Republic domestic manuals and architectural criticism underscored the masculine identity of the house, citing the negative consequences on national values if patriarchy were undermined. In *La Nouvelle Babylone* (1862) Eugène Pelletan sermonised that to 'save the fatherland' it was necessary to 'regenerate men at home'.[17] Wives were cast as sentinels of the house, charged with safeguarding morality against the myriad temptations beyond its walls and with orchestrating a feminine ambiance that would entice her husband to stay home. Sharon Marcus has argued that these discourses advocated the 'convergence of interiorisation and masculinity' as a way to maintain order and stability after the Revolutions of 1848 and 1871.[18] The power structure operative within the 'ideal' bourgeois family was given official endorsement in

Disdéri's oft-reproduced *carte-de-visite* of Napoleon III *en famille*. Set within props that bespeak domesticity, the Emperor appears upright in the forceful pose of patriarch, while his young son and heir apparent also stands aligned vertically with his father. With head bent, Empress Eugénie sits to one side, assuming a subservient posture in deference to the dominant males.[19]

Moreover, an emergent feminism heightened national anxiety associated with the usurpation of male hegemony, fears memorably satirised by Honoré Daumier as early as 1844 in his series *Les Bas Bleus* (*The Bluestockings*), printed in *Le Charivari* (fig. 1). The trouser-clad, bicycle-riding, cigarette-smoking *Femme Nouvelle* (*New Woman*) continued her threat to derail the 'natural' order of gender relations half a century later at the Feminine Congress, held in Paris (1900). In contrast, among the staples at the annual Salons were meticulously detailed domestic interiors that stressed the house as a feminine precinct where women were deployed as decorative objects amid men's other possessions. Paintings by James Tissot, Alfred Stevens, and Carolus-Duran, for example, often feature women ornamenting the home in the role of 'good wife' whose directive is to give pleasure to men. John House has noted that males make few appearances in academic paintings featuring middle-class dwellings. When men are portrayed 'their roles are made very explicit and conform closely to stock gender stereotypes',[20] thereby reinforcing male supremacy. Cautionary tales of domesticity gone awry abounded, however, in the trope of the 'fallen woman', underscoring the feminine mandate to maintain order and morality, not only within the home but, by extension, throughout the nation.

Impressionist interiors both intersect and subvert the prevailing discourse. Typically portraits of the artist's family and friends, these images are imbued with deep psychological resonances that bespeak intimacy with the sitters portrayed. Men are often revealed alone and ensconced within traditionally 'masculine' spaces, such as the study, or are situated in concert with women, thereby eliciting a subtly nuanced layering of 'male' and 'female' in space. At times the male presence is implied even when absent, conjured through the disposition of telling objects that serve as his metonymic substitute or in the figure of the unseen male artist poised as observer outside the frame. Equally revealing is what avant-garde artists chose not to paint from the many bourgeois rituals that were habitually enacted within the house. Deleted were social events, such as salons with invited guests or performances before a gathered audience, subjects favoured by Salon Naturalist painters like Tissot and Jean Béraud. Themes selected by Impressionists predominantly imply isolation and inwardness—listening to music, dining, reading, writing, painting, daydreaming. These works are iconoclastic in conjoining interiors and interiority, framing informal moments of daily life. Like an architectural section, Impressionist pictures shear the outer walls to uncover rooms purposefully hidden and beyond the reach of prying eyes. The composite portrait of masculinity conveyed is multivalent, individualised and self-absorbed.

The symbiosis between inhabitant and interior, whereby the dwelling is an analogue of its occupant, was a recurrent theme in poetry and novels of the period. Duranty aligned the 'New Painting' with Naturalist fiction, citing Honoré de Balzac as the progenitor of a congruency between dweller and dwelling place. Through vivid and evocative language, Balzac in his novels fuses person and place, the one an accurate incarnation of the other. Duranty similarly pronounced that 'the language of an empty apartment must be clear enough to enable us to deduce the character and habits of its occupant'.[21] Duranty attributed eloquence to material objects and settings that can be read in semiotic terms. Like clues in a detective novel—a literary form invented by Edgar Allan Poe that flourished during this period—objects provide signs that, when deciphered, unlock the internal workings of the protagonists. In Duranty's novella *Bric-à-Brac* (1876) pieces of furniture assume the physiognomy of their owners, denoting compatibility between people and things that recalls Edgar Degas's remark that a discarded corset still retains the form of the wearer.[22] Writing on the nineteenth-century interior, Benjamin likened the house to a shell that 'bears the impression of its occupant', who leaves upon it embodied 'traces'.[23]

During this period certain rooms were unequivocally male enclaves and the designated precincts to which men retreated after dinner, including the billiard room and the smoking room.[24] Degas's sensitive study of *The Billiard Room at Ménil-Hubert* (1892, Staatsgalerie, Stuttgart), the family home of his childhood friend Paul Valpinçon and often visited by the artist, is unusual in presenting a 'portrait' of an unoccupied space. The signpost of the room's 'male' gender is clearly the billiard table, just as the array of paintings that tastefully decorate the enveloping walls identifies the absent owner as a serious collector, another male purview. The table is animated in its rush to meet the rear wall through an exaggerated perspective recession that is more intuitive and experiential than mathematically measured. Additionally, the flattening effect of the stippled brushwork, signifying the rug, suggests that the floor is a tilted plane and unable to support the room's contents. Walls, furniture and even the heavily weighted table seem not to rest on *terra firma*. Despite being devoid of the requisite males, the room appears fully inhabited, suspended between moments of past and future time. Degas's image could be an exercise in Duranty's prescription that décor serve as a substitute for individuals. In *La nouvelle peinture* Duranty further observed that painting lacks the instantaneity of photography and relies instead upon a synthesis of moments, an inevitable combination of observation and memory that '*sums up* life'[25]

At the Piano

Invoking a seventeenth-century Dutch interior in the prose-poem 'L'Invitation au Voyage' from *Le Spleen de Paris,* Baudelaire anthropomorphised the room's contents and portrayed 'all furniture… armed with locks and secrets like all civilised souls…play a mute mysterious symphony for the eye'.[26] Seventeenth-century Dutch art provided an indispensable model of domesticity and of the suggestive collusion that bound figures and objects in a room. Connoisseur and critic Théodore Thoré spearheaded the revival of Dutch painters, specifically Johannes Vermeer, considered a master in manipulating milieu to comment subtly upon his characters. In an 1866 article in the *Gazette des Beaux-Arts*, Thoré singled out Vermeer's frequent exploitation of the pictorial device, the 'picture within a picture'. Analysing Vermeer's *Young Woman Standing at the Virginals* (c.1673-75, fig. 2), Thoré noted that the head of the musician overlaps a painting on the rear wall of Cupid holding a letter. Thoré 'read' the painting's subtext as Love and the absent male, embodied by his surrogate letter, literally occupying the woman's thoughts as she awaits her lover's missive.[27] Thoré's writings shaped the prism through which Vermeer and the 'petites maîtres' from the Low Country were viewed. In the process, the critic formulated the bourgeois interior as a performative space, a fitting setting for what Thoré called 'le petit drame' that pervades private life.

Despite his frequent absences, the male presence permeated the nineteenth-century home. In *At the Piano* (1858-59, fig. 3), James McNeill Whistler allowed musical instruments to function like poetic synecdoche, as substitutions for absent men. Sitting in the salon of her London townhouse, Whistler's half-sister, Deborah Haden, plays while her daughter, Annie, solemnly listens. Both are dressed in the colours of mourning. The piano belonged to Deborah's and Whistler's deceased father; its presence constituting a physical repository of childhood memories. Lying underneath the piano is a cello, a recognisably 'male' instrument during this period,[28] belonging to Deborah's husband, Seymour Haden, physician, collector of Dutch art and Whistler's mentor at the time. Borrowing a technique from stereoscopic photography, Whistler positioned the figures side-by-side on the same plane to amplify the illusion of depth through reverse perspective. The space of the room appears to advance visually, wrapping the figures, instruments and unseen artist in a sonorous atmosphere that reunites family members through music and memory. In painting and literature, the trope of a woman playing the piano followed specific, socially prescribed conventions that largely defined the player relative to the male observer. Michelle Perrot explains that in popular culture a solitary female pianist, 'hair down, face illuminated by candles, eyes vacant…was depicted as a prey to male desire'.[29] By contrast, Whistler's interpretation postulates parity between artist and sitters, a testimonial to their familial intimacy that fosters a fusion of subject and object. The personification of the piano and cello recalls the words of Albert, the protagonist in Théophile Gautier's story *Celle-ci et celle-là*: 'Poetry is everywhere…like a snail you are encased in your shell…this furniture and you are of the same substance…'[30]

Like Whistler's *At the Piano*, Degas's double portrait of his friends, *Monsieur and Madame Manet* (c.1868-69, fig. 4), thematises the dyadic relationship between player and listener, though now the pair consists of husband and wife. The room depicted is in Manet's mother's third-floor apartment on rue de Saint-Pétersbourg, the site of weekly salons where Suzanne Manet, an accomplished pianist, regularly performed and where the couple lived for several months. A gift to the sitters from Degas, the canvas was curiously slashed by Manet, reportedly in protest over Suzanne's unflattering image.[31] The remnant reveals a distracted and distant Manet casually posed and clearly unaware of being observed. Slouched on a sofa in the corner, Manet is connected to his wife through their overlapping forms—his left foot rests either beside or beneath the bottom fold of her gown—but inward-looking in his obvious self-reflexivity. Though facing in opposing directions, the two are joined spatially through music and the resonance that unites player and listener. While it was commonplace for musicians, particularly women, to entertain guests at domestic soirées, Degas decontextualises and isolates his

fig. 4. **Edgar Degas (1834-1917)**
Monsieur and Madame Edouard Manet, 1868-1869
Oil on canvas, 65 x 71cm
Kitakyushu Municipal Museum of Art

fig. 5. **Paul Gauguin (1848-1903)**
The Painter's Home, rue Carcel, 1881
Oil on canvas, 130.5 x 162.5 cm
The National Museum of Art, Architecture and Design Oslo

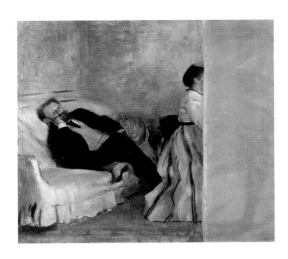

sitters, focusing instead upon their self-containment and the power of music to stimulate an interior journey. As Anne Leonard has observed, Baudelaire's 1861 essay in defence of Richard Wagner's *Tannhäuser* provided the model for inner, synesthetic listening,[32] whereby colours, smells and sounds interpenetrate. The poet wrote of feeling 'freed from the constraint of weight…I evoked the delectable state of a man possessed by a profound reverie in total solitude, but a solitude with vast horizons… immensity without other décor than itself'.[33] Degas revisited this theme in another double portrait of his father, Auguste, and the Spanish singer, Lorenzo Pagans (1871-72, Musée d'Orsay, Paris) that portrays a musical evening held in the salon of the De Gas family apartment at 4 rue de Mondovi. The artist's father, who reportedly 'drank in the music',[34] appears transported by Pagans's guitar, whose melody is evoked in the warm tone of the orange underpainting that emerges like a *pentimento* throughout the canvas to envelop both men. Musician and listener fuse in a morass of rich brown tonality that camouflages the contours of clothing separating their respective bodies. Though these images are specific to time and place, Degas invents a visual language that commemorates the home as a collaborator in the lived experience of its occupants, rather than as the scene of an historical event.

Paul Gauguin plays the dual roles of artist/observer and listener, inserting himself as the standing male in *The Painter's Home, rue Carcel* (1881, fig. 5, cat. 19), exhibited at the 1882 Impressionist exhibition under the title *Flowers, Still Life*. The room has been identified as the parlour in the Paris apartment the artist shared with his wife Mette, shown at the piano, and their children.

The couple and piano are sandwiched between a charcoal grey screen and dark rear wainscoting whose sombre tonality melds with the figures and piano. The screen divides the room into two separate but interpenetrating zones. The front area is dominated by an outsized glass vase of multi-coloured

zinnias that, together with a sewing basket and open book, earned the canvas its original title. These still-life elements distinguish the foreground from the musician and listener to the rear. The high-keyed colouration of bouquet and tablecloth expands this space perspectively, in contrast to the flattened corner into which figures and piano are slotted, initiating a dialogue between three-dimensionality and two-dimensionality. This segmentation of spaces suggests Baudelairean methodology whereby concrete objects in the visible world induce imaginative, interior travel through synesthetic suggestions. Stressing the significance of the still-life through the original title, Gauguin points the viewer to the vase of flowers as the visual starting point; its curve connecting optically to encircle the man, woman and empty chair, the latter an apparent invitation to the observer to enter the space mentally. Like Baudelaire's *Les Fleurs du Mal*, the flower's suggestive colours and emitted fragrances evoke sounds that move the viewer from the material to immaterial realms. Mostly hidden, the disembodied figures and piano appear as ethereal and abstract as music itself. Gauguin painted another view into this apartment, *The Little Dreamer*, (1881, cat. 25) in which a musical note can be deciphered amidst the birds that decorate the wallpaper. In his essay 'Synthetic Notes' (1884-85), Gauguin wrote: 'You are able to dream freely when listening to music, just as when viewing a painting'.[35] In these images the room is an incitement to dream and a container of sound, both real and metaphoric, that promotes inner listening and reverie.

Caillebotte's portrait of his brother Martial (1876, fig. 6) presents a rare instance of a male playing a piano within a domestic interior. Gloria Grooms has observed that critics identified the musician as a 'student of Marmontel', a well-known teacher, ascribing more serious commitment than attributable to a female whose amateur status would have been assumed.[36] Critics also responded to the instability conveyed by the massive Erard piano, shoehorned into a corner and 'not sufficiently propped up… one fears to see it fall at any instance on this nice young man'.[37] Surveyed from above, the room appears diagonally splintered into segments through the disproportionate scale change between the heavily weighted front versus the visually lighter rear of the piano, a disjunction also evident upon comparing the relative sizes of the two chairs.[38] Uniting the disparate parts are the curvilinear lines of plant tendrils growing rhythmically to cover drapery, carpets, wallpaper and curtains, visually connecting the room's patterns to the recursive lines visible on the sheet music upon which the pianist focuses. The 'feminine' lines of these decorative elements and chair silhouettes presage the later Art Nouveau sensibility, anticipated by the revival during this period of eighteenth-century Rococo aesthetics by Edmond and Jules de Goncourt.[39] A composer as well as a musician, Martial wrote music described as 'Wagnerian'.[40] In this image Caillebotte constructs a 'music-drama', a Wagnerian *Gesamtkunstwerk* or total work of art, blending sitter, space and listener—again invoked by the empty chair—into a seamless whole. Spatial distortions are expressive of subjective responses to highly charged rooms and subjects. Rather than simply optically accurate, the image achieves visual truth in evoking the resonance of the person, place and experience. In these images of musical listening, Whistler, Degas, Gauguin and Caillebotte open to the viewer, male or female, the possibility of re-experiencing the sensory, spatial and psychic interiors initially fashioned through the artist's interaction with intimate relations in familiar settings.

Male and Female 'At Home'

Conspicuous silence also frequently accompanied Impressionist pairings of male and female 'at home'. Private space, by definition, permitted the enactment of clandestine psychological and gender-related dramas, intended to remain closeted within the family. Avant-garde artists strikingly deviated from typical Salon practice, disdaining prescribed narrative formulas that ensured a painting's legibility. Instead their domestic scenarios relied heavily upon physiognomic and spatial cues that often disrupted viewer expectations or subverted cultural norms. During the nineteenth century physiognomic traits were a cultural fixation, obsessively scanned to categorise people by class and station and to negotiate interchanges between self and others. In everyday encounters subtle nuances of gesture, costume or decor assumed uncommon significance as modes of communication.[41] In *La nouvelle peinture* Duranty reinforced modernist painting's synchrony with contemporary experience in which 'states of mind' are articulated through the body, 'a back should reveal temperament… a gesture…an entire range of feelings'.[42] Resistant to easy closure, these views inside the house intrude upon privileged spaces, opening for inspection relationships normally hidden from outsiders and often difficult to 'read' definitively. Though typically recognisable in terms

fig. 7. **Edgar Degas (1834-1917)**
The Bellelli Family, c.1859-1867
Oil on canvas, 200 x 250 cm
Musée d'Orsay, Paris

of subjects and settings, Impressionist interiors can nonetheless remain hermetic, disjunctive, and open to a number of possible interpretations.

As the focus of family life, the house was the lightning rod for tensions that percolated behind its façade of public decorum. In an era when marriages were frequently arranged, divorce impossible, and women relegated to the status of minors under the law—necessitating dependence upon men for economic survival—strain within the conjugal unit was a fact of modern life.[43]

During the Second Empire the fiction of the harmonious family, with the father at the apex, was fundamental in buttressing societal stability. Nevertheless, the dysfunctional family was a recurrent theme in the literature of the period. Zola's novel of apartment living, *Pot-Bouille* (1884), reveals the subterfuge and intrigue at the core of modern marriage with the *maisons à loyer* or rented rooms contributing to domestic instability. Architecture theorist César Daly inveighed against the transience intrinsic to rented quarters incapable of fostering the merging of person and place guaranteed with a more permanent abode.[44] Similarly, in *Histoire d'une maison* (1873) Eugène-Emmanuelle Viollet-le-Duc critiqued apartment living, connecting stability and patrimony with the *hotel privée*, a vestige of patriarchy since the familial home was passed down from father to son.[45]

Edgar Degas's ambitiously scaled portrait the *Bellelli Family* (1858-67, Musée d'Orsay, Paris, fig. 7) reveals his beloved Aunt Laura, her husband Gennaro and their two young daughters posed within the Florentine apartment the family was forced to rent as a result of Gennaro's political exile from Naples. In a letter Gennaro admitted the humiliation he felt in needing to lease furnished rooms.[46] Degas, who lived with the Bellellis for several months, gives considerable weight to the room as symptomatic of emasculated male authority and marital discord. The palpable strain within the family is signalled by the position of Gennaro on the right, truncated and sandwiched into an impossibly compressed space between the chair and the mantle, and by the equivocal position of the central daughter poised between a towering mother and a shrinking father. The figures are locked within a grid-like armature of walls, doors and furniture whose cropped edges imply extensions beyond the canvas edge. Convoluted spatial compartments reflected in the mirror's illusory surface hint at psychic complexities masked by the detached, self-absorption of the figures. Like Whistler's

At the Piano, the painting encapsulates death within the image through objects that serve as substitutions for the deceased; in Whistler's case, the piano; in Degas's, the framed drawing of Laura's recently deceased father–Degas's grandfather–clearly outlined on the rear wall[47] and commemorated by Laura's black mourning clothes, as well as by the clock and flameless candles on the mantle, traditional *vanitas* emblems. Degas orchestrates strong dark tonalities that set the dominant thematic and emotional resonance of the interior which functions as more than a backdrop for human activities, but serves as an indicator of underlying psychological dynamics, the interior drama. The room's airless atmosphere recalls poet-critic Théophile Gautier's response to a domestic genre scene displayed at the Salon of 1853, 'you can *smell* the passing of the years as on opening a room closed since the death of a grandfather or great-uncle'.[48]

Degas again spatialised appreciable friction between male and female protagonists in *Interior* (1868-69, Philadelphia Museum of Art) and *Sulking* (1869-70, cat. 12), the former exploring the incursion of a male into an identifiably 'female' room, and the latter inserting a woman into a 'male' place of business. In *Interior* the man—standing like an alien intruder by the shadowed doorway of a bedroom and facing a partially dressed, seated woman—earned the painting its additional title, *Rape*. From its first appearance at Durand-Ruel Gallery in 1905, *Interior* has provoked much speculation concerning the derivation of its subject, with several literary sources by Naturalist writers proposed, among them Zola's novels of marital strife, *Madeleine Férat* and *Thérèse Raquin*. No conclusive evidence supports Degas's intention to illustrate any particular text, a testimony to the evocative, 'staged' quality of the image.[49] In her extensive analysis of this painting, Susan Sidlauskus offers an anti-narrative reading, stressing instead the empathic connection between viewer and space fashioned through the artist's manipulation of 'disturbing spatial anomalies that viscerally affect the spectator', arriving at a room 'at once claustrophobic and unprotected'.[50] The exaggerated perspective recession, together with the tipped floor plane, add to the dissonance between the couple, exacerbating female vulnerability and male aggression.

In contrast, the cropped fragment of a room framing the man and woman in *Sulking* intensifies their proximity to each other and to the viewer whose intrusion is acknowledged by the woman's outward gaze. Despite the relative closeness of the couple's bodies, a funnel-shaped void divides them, signalling an emotional rift as well. This gap is filled by a print of racing horses on the rear wall. Just as Vermeer had made revealing use of the 'picture-within-the-picture' motif, Degas exploits the agitated, arrested movements of leaping horses to denote the tangible tension that binds the pair. Deduced to be 'lovers or husband and wife', the woman has been assumed to be a 'visitor', presumably due to the 'male' designation of the room, identified by Theodore Reff as a banking office by the ledger rack and half-door.[51] The sitters are Degas's friend Duranty and a favourite model

fig. 8. **Gustave Caillebotte (1848-1894)**
Interior, Woman Reading, 1880
Oil on canvas, 65 x 80 cm
Private Collection

Emma Dobigny, but rather than portraits per se, the artist has manipulated the room and sitters, conjuring a dramatic encounter whose exact explication remains conjectural. Both *Sulking* and *Interior* sabotage the sanctity of gender-specific settings, concretising male/female discord through these spatial reversals.

Contemporary critics assumed that the man and woman in Caillebotte's *Interior, Woman Reading* (fig. 8) were a married couple and the painting a commentary upon the conjugal state. The disjunctive and, to some writers, even laughable perspective distortions were decoded as a visual critique of modern matrimony.[52] Most reviewers commented upon the noticeable scale discrepancy between the looming female in the right foreground and the dwarf-like male, swallowed up by the overstuffed sofa, in the background.[53] The palpable physical and spatial rupture between the couple, reinforced by the lines of wainscoting that box in each figure, was seen as evidence of their emotional estrangement. These jarring scale differences, together with each person's obliviousness to the other's presence, were not only interpreted as marital breakdown but also as the collapse of patriarchal order.[54] Critic and novelist J.K.Huysmans further commented upon the pair's respective reading material, taking his cue from their relative sizes. Without definitive visual evidence, Huysmans nevertheless concluded that the woman's corpulence indicated equally weighty reading matter—specifically the satirical political journal *Le Charivari* or the Republican newspaper *L'Évènement*—while her husband's diminutive proportions denoted lighter fare, such as a popular romantic novel.[55] To nineteenth-century viewers, reading carried specific gender connotations. Newspapers were considered an extension of the public realm and labelled 'male', while escapist fiction was deemed 'female'. Consequently a newspaper read by a woman, particularly while 'at home', signified an infiltration of masculinity into a feminine precinct, a meaningful reversal pursued in images by Mary Cassatt and Edouard Manet, among others. To the public these role reversals implied a weakening in the 'natural' hierarchy within the family, an attitude manifested in the critical response to this painting.

Berthe Morisot's portrait of her husband, *Eugène Manet on the Isle of Wight* (1875, cat. 23), may insinuate a wry commentary upon her newly-married state by inserting an obvious gender reversal. Leaning against the curvilinear rungs of a 'feminine' shaped chair,[56] Eugène turns his body to peer through a curtained window at a woman and child standing on the walkway beyond. Rather than a permeable membrane between interior and exterior spaces, the window in this image acts as a barrier that blocks access to the outside world. Eugène appears imprisoned behind the tangle of plants, grid of window panes and horizontal repetition of fence posts. Through the accentuation of these apparent obstacles, the male seems barred from egress and relegated to the role of spectator. By reversing the customary gendered spaces, Morisot appears to undercut the notion of the house as a purely feminine domain, mocking the trope of the 'bird in a cage', a common metaphor for women's place 'at home'. This image upends the observation made by Louise d'Alq, author of a homemaking manual for women, that 'the domestic hearth, the *at home*…occupies such an important place in life…that it always deserves…to be taken into serious consideration, especially by a woman, for whom it is her prison, or rather her nest, to use a slightly less harsh term'.[57] In recent years domestic interiors have been argued to be the particular province of female painters, since the restrictions placed on women precluded access to many public venues frequented by men.[58] Either through default or by choice, like their male colleagues women Impressionists mined the house as a nexus of modernity, inevitably coloured by the subjectivity at the heart of private life.

The dissonances that pervade these images differ markedly from the mood created by Edouard Manet in *Interior at Arcachon* (1874, cat. 22). In this room facing the sea, the symmetry between male and female connotes an easy familiarity that permits personal introspection and self-containment. Suzanne Manet looks up from her letter writing to the ocean viewed through the open window, while her son Léon pauses from reading or sketching. Both seem lost in thought and reverie, the literal space of the room affording a portal to figurative, imaginative spaces. In this work Manet presents a sharply contrasting, and infinitely more harmonious, view of male/female togetherness. Nevertheless, the present-day speculation relative to the actual paternity of Léon—rumoured to be the son of either Suzanne's husband Edouard or of Edouard's father, Auguste—itself points to the hidden turbulence sequestered behind the walls surrounding the bourgeois family.[59]

In the Study

Richard Wagner's 1867 music-drama, *Die Meistersinger*, represents his most potent meditation upon art and the creative process. In Act II archetypal artist Hans Sachs hones his craft in his 'workshop', an exterior space adjacent to the cobbler's home, that spills onto the Nürnberg street. Act III opens onto a softly illuminated room to reveal a contemplative Sachs seated alone at a table absorbed in the book he is reading. In this scene the dwelling offers asylum to the artist, a place of solitary contemplation and an invocation to reverie. Wagner's juxtaposition of outdoor and indoor spaces parallels the fluidity within Sachs's public/private, exterior/interior selves, implying that the layering of intrapsychic spatial compartments is critical to the creative process. The enclosed world of the interior, emblem of interiority, acts as a catalyst to making Art. Similarly, in the prose poem, 'La Chambre double', Baudelaire outlines the process of *dédoublement*, the making of doubles, which he considers the essence of creative expression. In one room, 'Une Chambre spirituelle', sentient furniture imbued with 'somnambulistic life' shares the poet's reverie and speaks to him a 'silent language'. Through an empathic fusion of subject and space, the room seems suspended within a time-free zone of 'clarity and the delicious vagueness of harmony', a utopian universe accessible via imaginative interiority. Intersecting and superimposed upon this idyll is its dystopic twin, a 'filthy hole, abode of eternal boredom'.[60] Baudelaire richly concretises his belief that from the collision of dualities—real/ideal, subject/object, finite/infinite, exterior/interior—Art emerges. The double rooms mirror the poet's split psyche whose projected subjectivity onto objective reality effects the latter's alchemical transformation into Art.

Numerous testimonials confirm the intimacy between the writer and his house, particularly his study. In a letter to a friend, Gustave Flaubert defined the sequestered spatial condition indispensable for him to write, 'You have to close your door and windows, curl up like a hedgehog, light a roaring fire in your fireplace because it's cold, and pluck some great idea from your heart'.[61] In Théophile Gautier's criticism and autobiographical sketches, the house served to cultivate creativity and trigger the aesthetic experience of the poet. Responding to a painting by Ernest Meissonier of a lone male writing in his study, Gautier delineated the process of empathic identification with the place. Moving from the minute specificities of the room to an absorptive daydreaming state that transcends time and space, he concluded, 'How conducive to meditation this solitude is…this good old room'.[62] Balzac produced what amounts to several hundred pages of correspondence delineating the furnishings and decoration of his residence, known as *Inventaire de l'Hotel de la rue Fortunée*, that rivals the painstaking recreation of interiors in his novels. Similarly, in his two-volume *La Maison d'un artiste*, Edmond de Goncourt devoted an entire chapter to the meticulous verbal recreation of each room in his house, amounting to a virtual tour of these private spaces. He explained that 'seated in the corner by a fire, enclosed and sedentary, the individual…wants the four walls of his *home* to be agreeable, pleasing, amusing to the eyes'.[63] The study, *Cabinet de travail*, comprises the most extensive chapter, spanning over three hundred pages of obsessive description of each 'book, manuscript and letter' in his well-stocked collection. Goncourt complained that 'life threatens to become public' and proposed the home, *le chez-soi*, as ultimate refuge.[64] For him objects set the stage for an inner journey of the imagination with one's home serving as a haven far removed from the mayhem and disorder of the streets. Surely the epitome of the writer in the study was Marcel Proust, cloistered within a cork-lined room that he rarely left as he penned *A la recherché du temps perdu*. As Diana Fuss explains, for Proust memory was 'built structure…

as much a spatial as temporal event'.[65] The domestic interior was the site of writing that suited the aura of contemplation and retreat that the house assumed. While commercial labour had been relocated to factory or office, the work of the writer remained 'at home' in the author's study.

Historically, the study was regarded as an exclusively masculine sanctuary, a place of privacy and autonomy for one person, associated with reading, writing and the male writer or scholar. Within the nineteenth-century bourgeois home, the study served as the seat of authority, the inner sanctum of the 'man of the house'. Woman's place at the hub of the household precluded the need for a solitary space which was considered inappropriate for a woman. Already by the eighteenth century the study had come to emblematise patriarchal supremacy, whereas the library became the principle room where women would go to read and write. Unlike the privacy afforded by the study, the library evolved into a decidedly social space. Victoria Rosner recounts that 'the overtones of power connected with private spaces of reading and writing were masculine…authorship, privacy and masculinity intermingled in the architectural genesis of the study'.[66]

Faithful to Duranty's prescription that an individual be situated within his characteristic environment, Degas's portrait of the author (1879, fig. 9) locates him in his study amid reams of paper and shelves of books.[67] In his review of the painting shown at the 1880 Impressionist exhibition, Huysmans notes that 'the person to be portrayed should be depicted at home…in a real setting… Here we see M. Duranty surrounded by his prints and his books, seated at his table, with his slender, nervous fingers, his bright mocking eye…'.[68] Degas's astute observation of objects and setting is matched by his insightful penetration into the writer's personality, conveying Duranty's intensity through his taut body and gestures. Caught seemingly unaware, the writer is absorbed in deep concentration at a private moment, in a familiar place. Akin to his other portrayals of men in their studies, including the writer Diego Martelli and the composer Pillet, Degas captured the enclosed nature of the room as an impetus to introspection and discipline, critical to the work of writing.

Manet thematised the intersection between the writer's study and his home in the *Portrait of the Poet Zacharie Astruc* (1866, fig. 10). The painting is dissected into two vertical sections. Astruc occupies the right side of the canvas and is seated beside a table arrayed with unevenly stacked books and a partly concealed quill pen—tools of the writer's trade—as well as a goblet and partially peeled lemon. In the upper left is the distant view of a domestic scene, comprising a woman leaning over a window sill and seen from the back, a rocking chair, thick curtain, plant and violin. The image merges work and home, the study immersed within an envelope of domesticity. The flowered tablecloth, fruit and glass near Astruc link the woman's domain with the male study. The background image, variously interpreted as a painting, mirror or another room, elides with the foreground 'study', making clear demarcation between near and far spaces ambiguous.[69] Manet visually implicates one zone as intricately connected

fig. 9. **Edgar Degas (1834-1917)**
Portrait of Edmond Duranty, 1879
Pastel and tempera, 100.9 x 100.3 cm
Burrell Collection, Glasgow, Scotland

fig. 10. **Edouard Manet (1832-1883)**
Portrait of Zacharie Astruc, 1866
Oil on canvas, 90 x 116 cm
Kunsthalle, Bremen

with and fuelling the other. Moreover, the image is rich with Baudelairean *correspondences*—smell, touch, sound— rooted in interior spaces and trigger to imaginative voyage.

In the Preface to *La maison d'un artiste* (1881), Goncourt set forth his intentions to write a 'memoir of things, of the milieu'. Second in scope only to the chapter on the study, the author devoted approximately one-hundred and fifty pages of meticulous description to his *Cabinet de l'extrême-orient*. This room housed his vast collection of Oriental figurines, porcelains and bronzes that testifies to the wide-spread collecting fervour for Japonisme during this period. Initially a piece of furniture used to store specimens assembled for scholarly study, so-called 'curiosités', the *cabinet* developed into a room with such furniture and eventually became subsumed into the male study.[70] Didier Maleuvre suggests that for the bourgeois dweller collecting represented 'a way of taking possession of the world...of domesticating the exotic...of securing the distant past...of enshrining personal memory'. Objects induce imaginative projection as time and geographic boundaries dissolve, 'the world is encapsulated in miniature form'.[71]

A mania for collecting gripped the nineteenth century, extending from authentic *objets d'art* to the mass-produced *bibelots*. In his *Étude sur Émile Zola*, Guy de Maupassant disclosed that Zola's bedroom in his Paris apartment 'is hung with ancient tapestries, a Henry II bed...old church stained glass windows cast myriad colours on a thousand fancy bibelots, quite unexpected in this den of literary rigor'.[72] Committed to scientific Naturalism in his novels, Zola nevertheless surrounded himself with an eclectic collection of furniture and art objects 'at home', amounting to a personally chosen survey of past times and far-off places. In his *Portrait of Émile Zola* (1867-68, Musée d'Orsay, Paris), Manet seated the writer at his desk surrounded by books and journals—noticeably the pamphlet Zola wrote in defence of Manet's controversial painting, *Olympia* (1863, Musée d'Orsay, Paris)—as well as several writing implements, including a porcelain inkwell and quill pen. Hanging on the rear wall are a lithograph after Velázquez's *Drinkers*, a *ukioy-e* print of a sumo wrestler by Kuniaki II, and a cropped Japanese screen—all influences on Manet's art—along with an etched reproduction of *Olympia*. These artworks span East and West, Old Master and Modern, implying a cosmopolitan taste that distinguished the painter as much as the writer. Such temporal and geographical admixtures reflect the synthetic process of making art and correspond to the idiosyncratic assemblage of objects that animate interior spaces. Zola's impassive face and far-away expression—so troubling to contemporary critics of the portrait[73]—convey self-reflection and interiority, activated by the room and its contents. Painted both in Zola's study and in Manet's studio, the portrait merges studio and study. Both rooms nurture its occupant and serve as stimulus to introversion and reverie.

In his review of Gauguin's painting, *The Painter's Home, rue Carcel*, Huysmans incorrectly identified the room as a 'studio interior', instead of the family parlour.[74]Huysmans's confusion suggests that not only was the domestic interior a subject of painting—thereby converting private space into an extension of the studio—but also that a visual correspondence aligned home and studio, making the studio an extension of home. Paintings of artists' studios reveal that in its décor the studio in many ways mimicked the house and, similar to the study, was an exclusively male enclave. Henri Fanin-Latour's documentary-like group portrait, *A Studio in the Batignolles Quarter* (1870, Musée d'Orsay, Paris) presents Manet seated at an easel surrounded by avant-garde painters and writers. All dressed in ties and frock coats, as if attending a domestic salon, the men, including Zola, Renoir, Astruc, Monet and Bazille, do not interact, but rather appear strangely detached from one another and stare in opposing directions. Framed pictures decorate the walls, and a Japanese vase and classically styled statuette of Athena ornament a table. Only the easel identifies this room as a 'studio'. A piano distinguishes Frédéric Bazille's *Studio in the rue de la Condamine* (1870, cat. 9), depicting a more informal gathering of his male colleagues, and includes furnishing and painting-lined walls that suggest the home of a collector or possibly an art gallery as much as a studio. Indeed public showings of Impressionist art were held in private galleries or apartments, whose intimate scale and furnishings aped domestic interiors.[75] The studio appropriated the dual aspects of the house, its more public side—midway between salon and café—and its private nature as a space that facilitates aesthetic contemplation and personal expression. In the latter aspect, the studio assumed the vestiges of home as generator of creativity, imagination, and subjectivity.

During the nineteenth century the term *intérieur* assumed a double meaning, signifying both the inner nature of the individual and interior space.[76] Walter Benjamin has argued that home as an expression of modernity comprised both these connotations, 'For the private individual, [the interior] represents the universe. In the interior, he gathers remote locales and memories of the past. His living room is a box in the theatre of the world'.[77] In France this new notion of domesticity and private life developed in response to immeasurable political, social and economic upheaval. During the heyday of Impressionism from the 1860s until the last group exhibition in 1884, being 'at home' in its most private regions served as an incubator for thought, imaginative voyage, and reverie, as well as the site of enactment of domestic dramas. Though designated a feminine domain, the masculine face of the modern interior has been chronicled by these painters, both male and female. Impressionist images of men in the house, performing the mundane activities of daily life, are neither mechanical transcriptions of milieu, nor dispassionate itemising of people, places and things. Like the rooms that enfold the sitters and the objects that act as collaborators with the protagonists, these paintings are constructions, shaped through the prism of artistic subjectivity that testify to the myriad ways that middle-class men were 'at home'.

1 See Michael Fried, 'Caillebotte's Impressionism', in Broude 2002, pp. 92-94.

2 Baudelaire 1975-76, vol. II, 'De L'Héroïsme de la vie moderne' *Salon de 1846*, pp. 493-96 and 'Le Peintre de la vie moderne', pp. 683-724.

3 See Marcus 1999, p. 136.

4 For an overview of the changes in the idea of private life, see Perrot 1990, Marcus 1999 and Forty 1986.

5 Duranty, reprinted in Moffett et al 1986, pp. 481-82.

6 Hemmings and Niess 1959, p. 73.

7 Moffett et al 1986, pp. 44-45 and p. 482.

8 Baudelaire 1975-76, vol. II, pp. 619-28.

9 Baudelaire 1975-76, vol. I, p. 11.

10 Baudelaire 1975-76, vol. I, pp. 287-88.

11 See Benjamin 1999, pp. 8-9, 19 and 21.

12 Benjamin uses theatre as a metaphor for the private realm when he writes that for the private individual the interior '… represents the universe…His living room is a box in the theatre of the world'. See Benjamin 1999, p. 19.

13 Moffett et al 1986, p. 482.

14 For a discussion of the house before the nineteenth century, see Perrot 1990, pp. 167-259.

15 For Adeline Daumard's speculation on the importance of the home, see Perrot 1990, p. 369.

16 Quoted in Berry 2006, p. 281.

17 Quoted in Stone 1995, p. 42.

18 Marcus 1999, pp. 135-39.

19 For a discussion of how photography formulated codes of presentation that came to carry semiotic meaning and illustrated behaviour considered appropriate for the myriad roles played by the 'self' see Alain Corbin, 'The Secret of the Individual' in Perrot 1990, pp. 460-66.

20 House 2004, pp. 16-17.

21 Moffett et al 1986, p. 482.

22 'Include all types of everyday objects positioned in a context to express the *life* of the man or woman—corsets that have just been removed, for example, and that retain the shape of the wearer's body'. Theodore Reff reprinted in Boggs et al 1988, p. 314.

23 Benjamin 1999, p. 220.

24 See Girouard 2005, p. 96.

25 Moffett et al 1986, p. 482.

26 Baudelarie 1975-76, vol. I, p. 302.

27 See Thoré 1866, p. 460.

28 The pose required to play the cello was deemed indecent for a young lady and remained the purview of the male musician. See Perrot 1990, p. 531.

29 Perrot 1990, p. 533.

30 Quoted in Snell 1982, p. 152.

31 See Boggs et al 1988, pp. 140-42.

32 Leonard 2007, pp. 266-86.

33 Baudelaire 1975-76, vol. II, p. 784.

34 Marcel Guérin reprinted in Boggs et al 1988, p. 171.

35 Prather and Stuckey 1987, p. 59.

36 Groom 1995, p. 193.

37 Louis Enault reprinted in Varnedoe 1987, p. 186.

38 The room seems a composite of different vantage points, implying the listener's movement in space and time.

39 See Silverman 1989, p. 25.

40 Varnedoe 1987, p. 64.

41 See Sennett 1978, p. 151.

42 Moffett et al 1986, pp. 481-82. See also Duranty 1867.

43 See Sidlauskus 2000, pp. 27-34 and Harvey 1985, pp. 152-54.

44 See Marcus 1999, p. 161.

45 For his views on domestic architecture, see Viollet-le-Duc 1987, pp. 246-380.

46 For information regarding Gennaro Bellelli and the circumstances surrounding his exile, see Baumann and Karabelnik 1994, p. 20.

47 Reff 1976, pp. 96-98.

48 Quoted in Snell 1982, p. 125.

49 For an overview of the literary texts proposed, see Boggs et al 1988, pp. 145-46.

50 Sidlauskus 1993, pp. 671-96.

51 Reff 1976, pp. 116-20.

52 '[The painting] greatly amuses visitors. A fat woman with purplish-red cheeks, sprinkled with rice powder, is seated and reads. Beside her, on a sofa that touches her chair, lies a man who is also reading. This man, her husband no doubt, is reduced to infinitesimal proportions... They have laughed a lot about Mr. Caillebotte's little husband'. Eugène Véron reprinted in Berson 1996, p. 317.

53 Henry Trianon compared the husband to a child's doll, his small stature made apparent when compared to the woman's large hand that touches his head. See Berson 1996, vol. 1, pp. 313-14.

54 For a discussion of critical responses to this painting, see Groom 1995, p. 204 and Broude2002, p. 143.

55 See Berson 1996, vol. 1, p. 287.

56 See Gloag 1973, p. 60.

57 Quoted in Marcus 1999, p. 152.

58 See Pollack 1988, pp. 50-90 and Parker and Pollack 1981. See also Janet Wolff's seminal essay, 'The Invisible Flâneuse', in Wolff 1990. I am arguing that the home was also the locus of modernity for men and a condition pursued by both male and female artists.

59 Locke 2001.

60 Baudelaire 1975-76, vol. I, pp. 280-82.

61 Letter from Gustave Flaubert to Maurice Schlesinger (April 1857). See Flaubert 1980, p. 701.

62 Quoted in Snell 1982, p. 125.

63 Goncourt 2003, vol. I, p. 2.

64 See Goncourt 2003, p. 104.

65 Fuss 2004, p. 7.

66 See Rosner 2005, p. 96.

67 For a summary of the parallels between Degas and Duranty, see Armstrong 1991, pp. 73-100.

68 Huysmans 1883, p. 117.

69 See Dolan 2006, p. 152, n 9.

70 McKeon 2005, pp. 225-28.

71 Maleuvre 1999, p. 115.

72 Maupassant, 'Étude sur Émile Zola', *Œuvres complètes*, 1908-1910, vol. 24, p. 165.

73 Paul Mantz and Jules Castagnary objected to Zola's blank expression. See Cachin, Moffet and Bareau 1983, p. 284.

74 Brettell et al 1988, p. 27.

75 Groom 1995, p. 179.

76 Larousse 1864-90, p. 88.

77 Benjamin 1999, p. 19.

Catalogue

1. Henri Gervex (1852-1929)

Café Scene in Paris, 1877
Oil on canvas, 100.5 x 136 cm
Founders Society Purchase, Robert H. Tannahill Foundation Fund,
Detroit Institute of Arts

Henri Gervex was an academic painter whose subjects ranged from the mythological to the modern life. He counted among his friends Impressionist painters such as Degas, who depicted him in *Six Friends at Dieppe* (1885, RISD Museum, Providence, Rhode Island) and Renoir, who included him in *La Moulin de la Galette* (1876, Musée d'Orsay, Paris). Gervex was also associated with Emile Zola, who partially based the fictional artist Fagerolles on him in his novel in *L'Oeuvre* (1886).

Café culture was an integral aspect of artistic life in nineteenth-century Paris. For many writers and painters, bohemians and conservatives alike, cafés became homes from home, where they could eat and drink cheaply, socialise and share ideas. The Irish writer George Moore who lived in Paris from 1873 to 1877 was a friend of Gervex and an ardent appreciator of cafés. He proudly declared 'I did not go to either Oxford or Cambridge but I went to La Nouvelle Athènes'.[1] According to Moore the Paris café was the only worthwhile 'Academy' of art.

Gervex depicts a group of men and women drinking and smoking at marble-topped tables. He presents himself at the centre of the composition, lighting a cigarette. The dramatist William Busnach sits beside Gervex, reading a newspaper and to the right is another friend, perhaps the painter Ferdinand Humbert or the poet Albert Mérat.[2] A woman in pink, most likely the artist's mistress Louise Valtesse de la Bigne, turns her back to the viewer. Beside her, a cigar smoking man has his 'head turned' by an enigmatic woman in black.[3] In this composition Gervex may have merged portrait studies and imagined characters to illustrate the 'types' who frequented Parisian cafés.

Aspects of this smoke-filled scene were directly inspired by Edgar Degas's *L'Absinthe* (1876, Musée d'Orsay, Paris), most obviously the glass of absinthe and its accompanying carafe of water that rest on the central table. The distant expression of the woman in black is also indebted to Degas's absinthe drinker.[4] Separated from the central group by a pillar, she sits alone, veiled and smoking a cigarette, all of which hint at her questionable moral status.

1 George Moore, *Confessions of a Young Man* (London 1952), p. 68.
2 Gourvennec 1992, p. 100.
3 He may be the newspaper publisher James Gordon Bennett Jr. Information provided by Detroit Institute of Arts.

4 Ellen Andrée, the model for *L'Absinthe*, later modelled for Gervex's *Rolla* (1878, Musée des Beaux Arts, Bordeaux).

2. Edouard Manet (1832-1883)

A Bar at the Folies-Beregère, 1881
Oil on canvas, 47 x 56 cm
Private Collection, courtesy of Pyms Gallery, London

This oil sketch is a preliminary study for Manet's enigmatic modern-life painting *A Bar at the Folies-Beregère*, which he exhibited at the Salon in 1882.[1] Here a blonde-haired *serveuse* stands behind a bar counter with her head turned towards a gentleman customer whose reflection, like hers, can be seen in the mirror behind.[2] The woman is positioned on a higher level as though standing on stage, and the artificial lights draws attention to her bright hair, décolletage and bare forearms. With hands clasped she awaits a cue from the diminutive, dapper customer, who wears a bowler hat and holds a gold-tipped cane to his mouth. Just under half the size of the Salon picture, this work is much looser in composition and darker in tone. It captures the theatre's shadowy sparkle with a restricted palette, comprised largely of black, white, yellow and brown. Despite ventures into landscape and seascape painting Manet, like Degas, was essentially a painter of the modern interior. He said to Berthe Morisot 'you can do *plein-air* painting indoors, by painting white in the morning, lilac during the day and orange-toned in the evening.'[3] This study of Parisian nightlife demonstrates effectively Manet's point.

Unlike outdoor café-concerts the Folies-Beregère charged its patrons an admission fee which lent a distinct exclusivity to the seedy delights of its smoky interior. There, the Parisian *demi-monde* gathered to eat, drink and socialise. In 1871 the theatre was refurbished dramatically and its auditorium transformed into a faux-Moorish winter garden complete with bars, fountains, promenades and mirrored walkways. The venue became a hybrid of interior and exterior; a pleasure garden and boulevard housed under a single roof. J.K. Huysmans celebrated its vulgar beauty as follows:

Edouard Manet (1832-1883), *A Bar at the Folies-Beregère,* 1882
Oil on canvas, 96 x 130 cm. The Samuel Courtauld Trust,
Courtauld Institute of Art Gallery, London

What is truly admirable, truly unique, is that this theatre has a real air of the boulevards about it. It is ugly and it is superb, it is both exquisitely good and outrageously bad taste. It is also unfinished like anything that aims to be truly beautiful.[4]

Manet has painted his theatre interior with an 'open air' eye. The figures on the balcony form a shifting landscape lit by the white glow of chandeliers and like the scene's orange tones and sketchy immediacy reinforce his belief that 'you can do *plein-air* painting indoors'.

1 *A Bar at the Folies-Bergère*, 1882, oil on canvas, 96 x 130cm, Courtauld Institute of Art Gallery.
2 The customer may have been modelled on the military painter Henri Dupray (1841-1909).

3 Comment from 1868-78 recorded by Morisot, quoted in Wilson-Bareau 2004, p. 203.
4 'The Folies-Bergère in 1879', Huysmans 2004, p. 43.

3. Edouard Manet (1832-1883)

The Ball at the Opéra, 1873
Oil on canvas, 36.5 x 28.5 cm
Private Collection, courtesy of Pyms Gallery, London

This painting is one of two known oil sketches that Edouard Manet made for *Masked Ball at the Opéra* (1873, National Gallery of Art, Washington). He began the finished painting in situ but spent many months working on it in his studio from life models and sketches before submitting it to the Salon of 1874, where it was refused by the jury. Although this oil study does not correlate exactly with any part of the finished painting, it demonstrates effectively Manet's driving motivation by presenting a visual slice of the fashionable crowds who attended the Opéra's annual masked ball.

Manet does not frame his composition to fulfil Academic expectations of symmetry and balance. Instead the urbanite crowd mills about the canvas as though independent of the artist's control, extending beyond its perimeters and edging forward into the viewer's space. The composition offers no primary pictorial narrative but instead a series of random encounters. In the middle distance a man enters the scene, his black cloak, like a crow's wing, arresting the movement of a masked woman in a dove grey domino. The casual intimacy of this interaction hints at the licentiousness of balls at the Opéra, a notorious venue for thinly veiled prostitution.

In the left foreground, a figure stands apart from the throng as if exiting the scene. Although the most clearly individualised and disengaged member of the crowd he is nonetheless part of it. In stylish dress-suit, he holds a cane in one gloved hand and places the other in his pocket. His shiny top-hat touches, overlaps and adds to the high horizon of chimneystack hats on anonymous heads. Manet has focused his picture upon a *flâneur*, the modern-city dweller celebrated by Charles Baudelaire:

> For the perfect *flâneur*, for the passionate spectator, it is an immense joy to set up house in the heart of the multitude, amid the ebb and flow of movement, in the midst of the fugitive and the infinite. To be away from home and yet to feel oneself everywhere at home; to see the world and to be at the centre of the world, and yet to remain hidden from the world.[1]

With deft strokes and patches of mono-chromatic colour, Manet depicts a melting mass of figures in the foyer of the Opéra. The *flâneur* standing among this disparate throng may represent the artist himself who felt most 'at home' in the public spaces of the modern city.[2]

Edouard Manet (1832-1833), *Masked Ball at the Opéra,* 1873
Oil on canvas, 59.1 x 72.5 cm. National Gallery of Art, Washington,
Gift of Mrs. Horace Havenmeyer in memory of her mother-in-law,
Louisine W. Havenmeyer

1 Charles Baudelaire, 'The Painter of Modern Life' (1863), Baudelaire 1995, p. 9.
2 For Manet's self-inclusion in the finished painting see Nochlin 1991, pp. 84-85.

4. Edgar Degas (1834-1917)

Café Concert at Les Ambassadeurs, 1876-1877
Pastel on monotype, 37 x 26 cm
Musée des Beaux Arts de Lyon

For a concentrated period between 1875 and 1880 Degas executed a number of prints and drawings based on the subject of the café-concert. These popular entertainment venues had existed in Paris since the 1840s but in the late 1860s were given licence to expand their repertoire to include plays, dance acts, acrobatics and costumed performers. This injected café-concerts such as the Alcazar d'Ete, Folies-Bergère and Moulin Rouge with a sense of spectacle that attracted Degas, Edouard Manet and Henri Toulouse-Lautrec and other artists of modern-life subjects.

This work is one of two pastel drawings executed over monotype prints entitled *Café-concert* that Degas exhibited at the third Impressionist group exhibition in 1877.[1]

It depicts a concert held at the celebrated Café des Ambassadeurs on the Champs-Elysées. In the summer months this café would hold its concerts under the trees, in an open-air pavilion that was lit by strings of full-moon shaped lamps. Degas takes his viewpoint from within the seated crowd, looking over the heads and hats of the audience and orchestra and towards the stage. There, at its very edge stands the singer Emélie Bécat in a flame-coloured dress. With exaggerated gestures, she stretches one hand towards the audience and with the other slightly raises her skirt, while undoubtedly performing one of the bawdily suggestive songs for which she was known.

Degas's pictures, more than those of any other Impressionist artist, are dominated by interior spaces. Working indoors best served his fascination with intimate figurative subjects. It was also necessitated by the eyesight problems he suffered from the early 1870s, which made it increasingly difficult to work in bright natural light. This night-time scene is an unusual amalgam of interior and exterior spaces, in which the stage's edge acts as a boundary between the two. The audience sits under trees in the open air, wearing outdoor clothing, bonnets and top-hats. The performers, by contrast, inhabit the stage like a vulgar parody of a society drawing room; an 'interior' that has been exposed to the elements and eager eyes. They wear short-sleeved muslin evening gowns and white gloves. One performer, in a blue dress, sits on an armchair and coquettishly raises a fan to her chin while scanning the audience for potential admirers.

Degas's application of bright pastels over a dark monotype print is, in a sense, an apt technique for an evening *en plein air* scene, in which the night is briefly coloured by artificial lights and the gaudy frocks of fleeting performers.

1 The related work is *Cabaret*, 1876/77, pastel over monotype, Corcoran Gallery of Art, Washington DC.

5. Edgar Degas (1834-1917)

In the Wings, c.1882-1885

Pastel on paper, 66 x 38 cm

Private Collection, courtesy of Pyms Gallery, London

Enthralled by the contrasts and contradictions of performance life, Degas engaged with the worlds of the ballet, opera and café-concert with the keen eye of an anthropologist. He produced hundreds of pastels, prints and paintings relating to the lives of ballerinas and cabaret singers. It was behind the scenes and in the wings that he uncovered and invented his most repeated subject of ballet dancers in their pre-performance states: apprehensive, bored, relaxing, preening and stretching.

This vividly coloured pastel depicts a young female singer standing at the stage side, awaiting her cue to perform. Holding a songbook loosely between her fingers she looks towards the stage where, above the flat brown reverse of the wings, we can glimpse its lights. The singer's simple costume, bare forearms and single silver bangle point to her youthfulness. Degas's inclusion of her companion, a top-hatted man in black who edges forward to overlap her body, highlights her naïveté. He is an *abonné*, one of the affluent annual subscribers to the Paris Opéra. These men enjoyed privileged backstage access, allowing them to move freely among, form relationships with and act as 'protectors' of the female performers. Although he focused mainly on the performers themselves, Degas occasionally included *abonnés* in his ballet compositions, their black columnar forms punctuating the pastel froth of dancers.[1] They are mostly portrayed as predatory observers hovering about the inner sancta of the Opéra. In the late 1870s Degas began working on a series of monotypes illustrating his friend Ludovic Halévy's stories about the sorry and often sordid backstage lives of dancers.[2] *In the Wings* is lighter in tone and mood than these murky monotypes but still the intrusion of the *abonné* upon the young woman's physical space hints that a seamier reality exists beyond the bright lights of the stage.

In 1889 Georges William Thornley (1857-1935) in collaboration with Degas published a lithograph of this pastel titled *L'Attente de la chanteuse*.[3] The word '*L'Attente*' might simply mean 'The Wait' but could also be read as 'The Suspense'. Another pastel titled *L'Attente* (c.1882, The John Paul Getty Museum) similarly conveys Degas's fascination with private interiors behind public performance spaces. It depicts a seated ballerina waiting either before or after an audition.[4] *In the Wings* (*Dans les Coulisses*) is unusual in Degas's oeuvre as the artist more commonly depicted singers mid-performance and dancers behind the scenes.[5]

1 In *Ballet* (1871, pastel on paper, Musée d'Orsay, Paris) an *abonné* waits in the wings while the star ballerina performs, his head cropped out of view, and in *Dancers Backstage* (1876/83, oil on canvas, National Gallery of Art Washington) another edges towards a dancer who stands with folded arms.
2 Halévy's stories were published individually between 1870 and 1880 and as a collection under the title *La Famille Cardinal* in 1883. For a discussion of the complex publication history of the prints see Michael Pantazzi, 'Degas, Halévy, and the Cardinals', Boggs et al, *Degas*, exh. cat., (1988), pp. 280-84.

3 Published in *Quinze Lithographies d'apres Degas* by Boussod Valadon, an edition of 100 (plus 25 proofs signed by both artists), printed by Atelier Becquet, Paris.
4 Thomson, 1995.
5 An intriguing 'behind the scenes' depiction of a singer is *Before the Curtain Call* (1892, pastel on paper, Wadsworth Athenaeum). The singer is pictured on a carpeted set from a high viewpoint as an assistant arranges her costume.

6. Edgar Degas (1834-1917)

Two Ballet Dancers in a Dressing Room, c.1880
Pastel on paper, 48.5 x 64 cm
National Gallery of Ireland

From the 1870s Degas observed and recorded the movements of ballet dancers in over a thousand drawings, paintings, prints and sculptures. Through occasional backstage visits and the employment of young dancers (known as '*petit rats*') as models in his studio, he made endless sketches and observational notes to form a vast visual lexicon of movements and gestures. It was not until 1885 that he gained privileged *abonné* status, which allowed him to move freely behind the scenes of the Paris Opéra.[1] In the early 1880s, around the time he executed this pastel, Degas wrote to a collector friend Albert Hecht:

> Have you the *power* to get the Opéra to give me a pass for the day of the *dance examination*, which, so I have been told, is to be on Thursday? I have done so many of these dance examinations without having seen them that I am a little ashamed of it.[2]

Observed from a high viewpoint this scene features two dancers in a dressing room. Their layered white dresses, tied with blue sashes, are those typically worn by dancers in Degas's rehearsal scenes.[3] A selection of costumes hanging in the background forms a 'curtain' behind them; among these a tutu coloured with bold dashes of red, black and gold suggests that the dancers may be preparing to go on stage. The dancer on the left places her hands under her sash as though adjusting it for a costume change.[4] Her companion leans upon a simple wooden chair, perhaps tired from rehearsals and snatching a moment's rest before the performance. She holds a piece of semi-transparent fabric like a chiffon neck-scarf. On a rudimentary sideboard rests a bowl, and the cut-off forms of a jug and blue glass or goblet. Although carpeted and therefore relatively luxurious, the room is cramped and functional, an intimate enclosure designed for quick changes rather than relaxation.

Degas's pastels depicting the everyday occupations of ballerinas in rehearsal and dressing rooms echo the spontaneity of Impressionist landscapes by Monet, Pissarro and Sisley. The ever-shifting forms of these dancers, in airy white costumes, populate the drab landscapes of their 'shoe-box' rooms like a series of passing clouds.

1 In 1883 Degas was given a shared permit with artist Jacques Emile Blanche. Until then he had relied on influential friends for access backstage. Loyrette 1989, pp. 50-51.
2 Degas 1947, no. 43, p. 66.

3 Richard Kendall describes the scene as 'the moment when the members of the *corps de ballet*, having put on their stockings, dance shoes and tutus, wait for the call to the stage or idly rearrange their clothing', Kendall 1989, p. 48.
4 Lillian Browse identified this dancer as Mlle Salle. Browse 1949, pp. 396-97.

7. Edgar Degas (1834-1917)

Two Harlequins, c.1885

Pastel on paper, 32 x 24 cm

National Gallery of Ireland

The juxtaposition of brilliantly costumed performers with the mundane interiors of rehearsal spaces was a source of deep fascination to Degas. Here in a playful inversion of the bourgeois family interior, he shows two harlequin 'brothers' engaging in discussion, one seated while the other bends forward towards him. Their gestures convey an ease and intimacy indicative of the long hours that dancers spent living and working in each other's company.

The distinctive masked figure of the harlequin appears in only seven known pastels by Degas. This work, like the others, was inspired by a contemporary production of *Les Jumeaux de Bergame*. The original play by Jean-Pierre Claris de Florian (1782) was adapted as a *ballet-arlequinade* by Charles Nuitter and Louis Mérante and premiered in the Paris Opéra on 26 January 1886.[1] Although this pastel pre-dates the opening performance, Degas is known to have attended rehearsals for the ballet in July 1885.[2] Indeed, the wooden chair and the simple background of what appear to be green window shutters and a poster (perhaps a set design) on the wall indicate that this is a rehearsal space.

Although rather androgynous in physique, the harlequins in this composition are in fact female travesty dancers.[3] They wear the colourful diamond-patterned leotards, black masks and dark caps associated with their *Commedia dell'Arte* characters. *Les Jumeaux de Bergame* told the story of two Harlequin brothers, Senior and Junior, who fell in love with the same woman. In one scene the character of Harlequin Senior unknowingly attacks Harlequin Junior with his baton after hearing him serenade his beloved. In this pastel the standing figure holds a baton denoting her role as Harlequin Senior. The chief characteristics traditionally ascribed to the Harlequin were agility and acrobatic skill. Here however Degas turns once again to the favoured motif of dancers resting, mid-rehearsal. These harlequins sit and lean upon a shared chair at the edges of a restricted space.

1 Browse 1949, pp. 58, 392-93.

2 Degas executed a number of harlequin pastels prior to the ballet rehearsals of July 1885. Gary Tinterow suggests that he may have been aware of an operatic version of *Les Jumeaux de Bergame*, devised by William Busnach in 1875, which featured ballet sequences. See Tinterow in Boggs et al 1988, pp. 431-34.

3 For a discussion of the travesty dancer in nineteenth-century ballet see Garafola in Ferris 1993, pp. 96-106.

8. James Jacques Tissot (1836-1902)

Women of Paris: The Circus Lover, 1885
Oil on canvas, 147.3 x 101.6 cm
Courtesy, Museum of Fine Arts, Boston, Juliana Cheney Edwards Collection

From 1871 to 1882, James Jacques Tissot lived in London, where he established a lucrative career as a painter of modern genre subjects. On returning to Paris he embarked upon an ambitious scheme of paintings entitled *Women of Paris*.

Unlike his friend Edgar Degas, Tissot did not aspire to paint scenes depicting the lives of Parisian laundry workers or ballet dancers. Instead he focused on the imagined and idealised figure of 'La Parisienne', the chic, confident and coquettish female believed to be unique to the French capital.

The Circus Lover (originally titled *Les Femmes du Sport*) is one of the fifteen large paintings that Tissot devised in the *Women of Paris* series. The women depicted were intended to act as genteel 'guides' to Paris's sights and entertainments, its shops, balls, circuses and parks. Tissot had such confidence in his idea that he planned to publish engravings of the paintings and accompany each with by a specially commissioned story or poem by a French writer.[1]

In this work Tissot depicts an audience of elegant Parisians enjoying a trapeze display at the Cirque Molier. This eccentric venue was set up by the entrepreneur Ernest Molier at his Paris home in 1880. An amateur circus, its entertainment was provided by aristocrats who entered the ring in the place of professional acrobats.[2] Here Tissot shows the celebrated Count Hubert de la Rochefoucauld sitting proudly on a trapeze.[3] Eager to be the centre of attention, he looks towards the women in the foreground. His monocle comically highlights his balancing powers. The circus interior is crammed with men in dress suits and top hats and women in fashionable attire. While the women regard the performance with interest the men are decidedly unimpressed with the acrobatics. Instead, they leer over the shoulders of women in the audience or peer at them through binoculars. The woman in the foreground dressed in a stylish pink gown is Tissot's 'Parisienne'. Looking from the picture with an air of ennui, she folds her fan to reveal herself and to reciprocate the gaze of the 'admirer' before her, namely the viewer of the picture. Effectively, Tissot portrays the Parisian woman as one of the city's most alluring spectacles.

---

1 Tissot commissioned Charles Yriarte to write a story for this painting however, the plan to publish poems and tales did not come to fruition.

2 The circus ran until Molier's death in 1934.

3 In 1885 *The New York Times* reported that Parisian society found newspapers 'flat, stale and uninteresting' but 'hankers after great sensations' such as 'the intended appearance of Count Hubert de la Rochefoucauld on the tightrope'. 'Paris Topics of the Day', 17 August 1885, p. 5.

9. Frédéric Bazille (1841-1870)

The Artist's Studio, rue de La Condamine, 1870

Oil on canvas, 98 x 128.5 cm

Musée d'Orsay, Paris, France

Bequeathed by Marc Bazille, brother of the artist 1924

Frédéric Bazille briefly attended the studio of Charles Gleyre between 1862 and 1863. It was during this time that he struck up friendships with the future Impressionists Claude Monet, Alfred Sisley and Auguste Renoir. These friendships extended beyond Gleyre's studio (which closed in 1863) to Chailly, near the forest of Fontainebleau, where they indulged a mutual love of painting *en plein air*.

Bazille, who was from a wealthy background, moved in to a large studio at 9 rue de La Condamine in January 1868, which for a time, he shared with Renoir. It was there that he painted this group portrait of his friends in 1870, just months before he was killed in the Franco-Prussian War. The room is large and airy; lit by an expansive window and heated by a small pipe stove that highlights the owner's Bohemian credentials.

The young artists are depicted in an easy and informal manner, engaging in discussions about art. The identities of the figures have not all been confirmed but have been suggested to be: Sisley or Renoir sitting on the table, Monet or Emile Zola on the stairs, Bazille at the easel holding a palette, Manet examining the canvas and behind him either Zacharie Astruc or Monet. Removed from the conversations, Edmond Maître plays piano in the corner. The furnishings are elegant but functional, the piano adding a note of luxury, reinforcing the sense that Bazille and his friends felt 'at home' in this bright bourgeois-bohemian space.

The features of these artists are well-known through portraits and self-portraits but the fact that they have not been identified with certainty perhaps highlights the easy interactions that artists within Bazille's circle enjoyed. Their relaxed attitude to artistic exchange is exemplified by Manet, who took Bazille's brushes and painted his tall figure into the portrait.

The informality of Bazille's studio interior is all the more explicit if one compares it to Henri Fantin-LaTour's *A Studio in the Batignolles Quarter* (1870, Musée d'Orsay, Paris). Painted in the same year, this work also depicts Manet, Renoir, Zola, Astruc, Monet and Maître but presents them in a formal static and 'silent' arrangement.

10. Edgar Degas (1834-1917)

Portraits in a Cotton Office (New Orleans), 1873

Oil on canvas, 73 x 92 cm

Pau, Musée des Beaux-Arts

Painted while Degas was visiting family in New Orleans, this picture was exhibited in 1876 at the second Impressionist exhibition.[1] The scene is set in the cotton offices part-owned by Degas's uncle Michel Musson.[1] An exclusively male environment, the interior is populated by clerks and customers and also features the artist's brothers Achille (leaning by a window) and René (reading *The Daily Picayune*) and his uncle (seated in the foreground). Each figure has a clear role to play, whether active, contemplative, talkative or observant. As visitors to their uncle's offices Degas's brothers assume informal, relaxed poses; René's posture would be just as appropriate in a parlour, while Achille could easily be propped at a café counter. Michel Musson acts as a paternal figurehead. Preoccupied in assessing a package of cotton, he is 'at home' in his workplace. His engagement with the material anticipates the many images of women sewing, knitting and weaving painted by Impressionist artists.

In 1876 critics observed that Degas's detailed finish was influenced by the work of Flemish and Dutch Old Masters. However, his inventive arrangement of the figures was regarded as innately modern. Edmond Duranty remarked:

'In actuality, a person never appears against neutral or vague backgrounds. Instead, surrounding him and behind him are the furniture, fireplaces, curtains, and walls that indicate his financial position, class and profession. The individual will be at a piano, examining a sample of cotton in an office, or waiting in the wings for the moment to go onstage, or ironing on a makeshift worktable.'[2]

Degas organised the pictorial space with both artistic licence and mathematical precision, merging real and invented elements. The apertures and recesses of sash windows, doorframes and shelves combine to give a sense of the shifting screens and backdrops associated with set design. Degas's manipulation of geometrical shapes and the layering of monochromatic figures are informed by Japanese ukiyo-e prints.

This picture was painted with a very specific market in mind. Degas wrote to Tissot saying that he planned to send it to the British dealer Agnew's with a Manchester cotton spinner and art-collector, William Cottrill, in mind as a purchaser.[3] *Portraits in a Cotton Office* could be regarded as a genre-piece conceived in the English illustrative vein; to be examined, scrutinised and quantified like the cotton itself. A business-like interior designed for a collector who appreciated both the business of art and the business of cotton.

---

1 Degas stayed in New Orleans from October 1872 until March 1873.
2 Duranty quoted in Moffett at al 1986, p. 44.

3 Letter from Degas to James Tissot, 18 February 1873, Degas 1947, p. 30. The painting was purchased by the City of Pau in 1878.

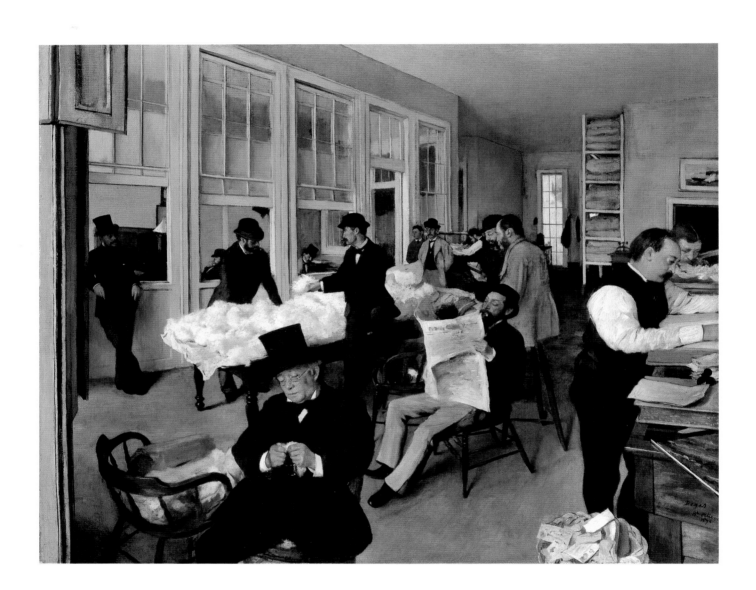

11. Louis-Joseph Anthonissen (1849-1913)

Ironing Workshop in Trouville, 1888

Oil on canvas, 61 x 83 cm

Pau, Musée des Beaux-Arts

The Belgian artist Louis Joseph Anthonissen trained at the Academy d'Anvers before attending the Ecole des Beaux-Arts in Paris. Primarily a painter of Orientalist subjects, Anthonissen regularly exhibited Algerian landscapes and genre scenes at the Salon de la Société Nationale des Beaux-Arts. *Ironing Workshop in Trouville* is an unusual subject for Antonissen but as the artist was a visitor to Trouville it would have been in tune with his keen interest in depicting 'foreign' lives.

The ironing workshop is located in a cramped garret lit by a single skylight and an open window. All that can be seen outside are rows of roofs and distant treetops. The laundresses stand with heads bowed over trestle tables pressing down upon the garments. Their rolled-up sleeves and pink cheeks indicate the steamy heat of the workshop. Above their heads hang criss-crossing lines of clothing: stockings, undergarments and sailor-style bathing costumes. It is not the view but these nautical suits that remind us that the scene is set in the seaside town of Trouville. The development of the railway helped transform this fishing village into a fashionable tourist resort, which was visited by artists such as Eugène Boudin, Gustave Courbet, James Whistler, Edouard Manet and Claude Monet, who honeymooned there in 1870. While these artists typically painted the seashore, stylish holidaymakers and the atmospheric effects of sunshine and sea breeze, Anthonissen looked indoors and undoubtedly to the urban laundry interiors of Edgar Degas for inspiration.

The worlds of women at work were central to Degas's oeuvre. His depictions of dancers, milliners and laundresses inspired contemporaries, Impressionists and others, to explore the everyday lives of modern women. Degas began depicting individual laundress figures in the late 1860s but by the 1880s had started to portray groupings of women ironing between hanging lines of linen.[1] Laundresses were commonly considered morally lax characters who were disposed to drinking, worked half-dressed and supplemented their pitiful incomes by casual prostitution. Degas's friend Emile Zola conveyed the miserable drudgery of the laundry worker's existence in his naturalist novel *L'Assomoir* (1877). Degas's laundry workers had a far-reaching impact upon contemporaries both with Academic and avant-garde affiliations. His scenes inspired artists as diverse as Anthonissen and Pablo Picasso, whose *Woman Ironing* (1904, Guggenheim Museum, Thannhauser Collection) introduces the motif with a world-weary weight into the twentieth century.

1 In 1876 Degas exhibited five *blanchisseuses* based pictures at the second Impressionist exhibition.

12. Edgar Degas (1834-1917)

Sulking, c.1870

Oil on canvas, 32.4 x 46.4 cm

The Metropolitan Museum of Art,

H.O. Havemeyer Collection,

Bequest of Mrs H. O. Havemeyer, 1929

Painted c.1870, this picture remained in Degas's studio until placed on deposit with the art dealer Durand-Ruel in 1895 as *Bouderie*.[1] Just as in *Interior* (1868/69, Philadelphia Museum of Art) and *The Song Rehearsal* (1872-73, cat. 18), the interactions within this interior scene are strained but suggestive. The title provokes investigation of the subject matter but does not provide a conclusive interpretation.

A man sits at a paper-strewn desk with his body turned and eyes averted from his female companion.[2] Resting her body over a chair-back and holding a small paper scroll tied with black thread, the woman looks directly out from the picture. Her relaxed pose might suggest the comfortable familiarity of a domestic context but the furnishings appear more appropriate to an office, study or perhaps a bank.[3] Above the man's head is a shelf of files, below which hangs a framed certificate of achievement or authority. These details, like the counter and panelled wall, are more befitting of a workspace than a parlour.

A large horseracing print – a colour engraving after *Steeple Chase Cracks* (1847) by the English sporting painter J.F. Herring Sr (1795-1865) – dominates the space between the couple's heads. The man and woman turn their heads in the opposite direction from the cantering horses, emphasising the stasis in their interaction. It is tempting to read this print as a connecting factor between them. Is the woman perhaps collecting winnings from a sullen bookmaker? In 1894 George Moore published his highly successful novel *Esther Waters*, in which the eponymous heroine is seduced by a bookmaker who is ultimately ruined by his penchant for horse racing. Perhaps Moore's recent literary triumph prompted Degas to consign this picture, which had been in his studio for so many years, to Durand-Ruel.

In the early 1870s Degas was deeply fascinated by English genre painting, with its descriptive detailing and focus on anecdotal and literary subjects. In *Sulking* he depicts material items such as furnishings and costumes in a highly finished manner but, by contrast, populates the space with enigmatic protagonists.

1 In 1898 Degas purchased Gauguin's *Te faaturuma* (1891, Worcester Art Museum, Massachusetts), which is often known as *The Brooding Woman* or *Sulking*.

2 Degas based these figures on the model Emma Dobigny and the art critic Edmond Duranty.

3 Boggs et al 1988, p. 147.

13. Zacharie Astruc (1835-1907)

Parisian Interior, 1874
Watercolour on paper, 36.4 x 28.4 cm
Musée d'Evreux

The writer, watercolourist and sculptor Zacharie Astruc is best-known as an art-critic and as a champion of Edouard Manet.[1] He keenly engaged with Japanese and Spanish art and was partially responsible for encouraging Impressionist and other avant-garde artists to look to these influences for inspiration. Despite his steadfast support of Manet, Astruc's paintings were, by contrast, highly conservative in subject matter and execution. He exhibited regularly at the Salon but in 1874 joined with the Impressionists to exhibit at their first group show.[2] Among the works he showed there was this small watercolour *Intérieur Parisien*, framed as one of a group of six pictures: *Dames flammandes a leur fenêtre*, *Scène de Somnambulisme*, *Enfants flamands dans une serre*, *Poupées japonaises* and *Les Présents chinois (Londres)*. Despite the naïve quality of these watercolours (indicative of Astruc's lack of formal art-training) they were positively received by critics who commented on their brilliancy of colour.

A woman seated on a *fauteuil confortable* is depicted within a highly decorated bourgeois interior. Set in the corner of a Parisian apartment, Astruc's composition resembles an open-sided doll's house. Every surface of the room is draped or masked in materials of contrasting colours and patterns: the *porte-fenêtre* is hung with velvet curtains held by tasselled ties, a floral carpet covers the floor, the stools and chair are variously upholstered, studded and fringed, the walls are peppered with pictures, and even the book resting on the footstool is leather-bound and metal-clasped.[3] This Parisian interior displays the urbane tastes of its inhabitants. The pictures suggest it may be the home of an art-lover. The portrait above the vase; a reduced copy after Bartolomé Esteban Murillo (1618-82) points to a fashionable interest in Spanish art of the Golden Age. Amongst the bric-à-brac and objets d'art the woman sits holding an oriental fan, her head aside as though in reverie.[4] This picture anticipates Edmond Duranty's comment on the representation of domestic interiors in modern painting: 'a person never appears against neutral or vague backgrounds. Instead surrounding him and behind him are the furniture, fireplace, curtains, and walls that indicate his financial position, class and profession. The language of an empty apartment must be clear enough to enable us to deduce the character and habits of its occupant'.[5] Astruc's interior inventories decorative details but like the work of Impressionist associates is distinctly devoid of anecdotal narrative.

1 In 1863 he famously defended Manet's exhibits at the S*alon de Refusés*: 'Le Salon des Refusés', *Le Salon*, 20 May 1863, p. 5. Manet quoted Astruc's poem 'Olympia, la fille des îles' in his 1865 Salon catalogue entry for *Olympia* (1863, Musée d'Orsay) and in 1866 painted his portrait (Singletary, fig. 10).
2 The group was then known as the *Société Anonyme de Artistes, Peintres, Sculpteurs, Graveurs, etc.*

3 Walter Benjamin astutely identified a peculiarly nineteenth-century phenomena of enveloping and encasing objects and inhabitants within domestic interiors. Benjamin, 'The Interior, The Trace' in Benjamin, 1999, [14.4], pp. 220-21.
4 Astruc had planned a series of works depicting the day-to-day lives of modern Parisian women. Flescher 1978, p. 424.
5 Duranty, 'The New Painting' (1876) in Moffett et al 1986, pp. 44-45.

14. Wilhelm Trübner (1851-1917)

On the Sofa, 1872
Oil on canvas, 52 x 45 cm
Staatliche Museen zu Berlin, Nationalgalerie

The German Realist painter Wilhelm Trübner was a student at the Kunstacademie, Munich when the International Art Exhibition took place at the Glaspalast in 1869. This unprecedented exposure to modern art and particularly the work of Courbet and Monet had an enduring impact upon the young artist and his associates. Courbet visited Munich during the exhibition and complained that the old guard of German painters was fixated with perspective, historical costume and anecdotal subjects chronicling royal events. By contrast, he observed 'the young people in Munich are doing well. I stayed a little longer for that reason. They have decided to abandon all the old relics. I saw some young painters spit on the floor when they spoke of all the princes of German art.'[1] Around this time Trübner became associated with a group of artists centred round the Realist painter Wilhelm Liebl (1844-1900).[2] It is undoubtedly to this group, who embraced enthusiastically the directness of French avant-garde art that Courbet refers.

Trübner painted *On the Sofa* in April 1872 in his native Heidelberg at a time when he was deeply influenced by Liebl's belief in the truthfulness of direct painting. A young woman sits on a small sofa and appears to have placed a book aside while she eats. She looks directly out of the canvas, echoing the unblinking gaze typical of Manet's models. On the table beside her rests a loose bunch of spring flowers and a glass vase holding a simple arrangement of lily-of-the-valley. The woman is soberly dressed and still in expression, as if part of a still-life composition. Her black dress and ruffled collar hint at the work of Dutch and Flemish painters of the seventeenth century whose realism was admired by the 'Liebl circle'. In a more modern context Trübner's realism echoes Degas's reinterpretation of past masters in his portrait *The Bellelli Family* (1858-67, Singletary, fig. 7).

The self-containment of the girl contrasts startlingly with the clashing patterns, textures and colours that decorate her surroundings. The blue wallpaper with its dense floral print, the white tasselled sofa covering, the chequered table-cloth and red-brown swirls on the rug, collide and clamour for attention. By the 1890s Trübner had become a keen advocate of Aestheticism. The absence of narrative and the decorative directness of this early painting signal his future fascination with formal aestheticism and theories of 'Art for Art's Sake'.

1 Letter from Gustave Courbet to Jules Castagnary, 20 November [1869], quoted in Chu 1992, pp. 355-56.

2 Forster-Hahn, Françoise, et al. 2001, pp. 154-65.

15. Camille Pissarro (1830-1903)

Minette, 1872
Oil on canvas, 45.9 x 35.6 cm
Wadsworth Atheneum Museum of Art, Hartford, CT
The Ella Gallup Sumner and Mary Catlin Sumner Collection Fund

Camille Pissarro was the only artist to exhibit at all eight Impressionist exhibitions between 1874 and 1886. He was primarily a painter of landscapes, and with the exception of occasional still-lifes, rarely painted subjects set in interiors. In contrast to Degas, Pissarro did not base his figurative paintings on the inhabitants of the modern metropolis but instead on the agricultural labourers who worked in the fields round his home in Pontoise.

This portrait depicts the artist's daughter, Jeanne-Rachel (b.1865), who was affectionately pet-named 'Minette'. Pissarro painted this work as a gift for his friends Ludovic and Adèle Piette in 1872. This couple had taken in the artist and his family when Prussian troops occupied their village of Louveciennes during the Franco-Prussian War in 1870. The family fled to London shortly afterwards. On returning to France in 1871, Pissarro found that Prussian soldiers had destroyed all but a few of his early paintings.

Pissarro has painted the portrait with a direct naturalism in order to convey the innocence of the little girl, for whom the Piettes had developed a strong affection. Minette wears country clothing with a rustic smock covering her dress and trousers, and a scarf knotted around her neck. Her shoes are simple and worn. She stands in the corner of a room next to a table on which one can see a silver coffeepot, a glass carafe and a decorated urn. Behind these decorative objects rests a bottle of wine on a ledge. This unsophisticated still-life arrangement most likely represents the sum total of the family's material 'treasures' after the war. Pissarro depicts his daughter as a cherished possession within the family home. The portrait is particularly poignant when one considers that Minette died at the age of nine, two years after it was painted. Following her death Ludovic Piette returned the picture to her father.[1]

---

1 Pissarro 2005, vol. 2, cat. 282, pp. 223-24.

16. Pierre-Auguste Renoir (1841-1919)

Young Woman in White Reading, 1873
Oil on canvas, 35 x 27 cm
National Gallery of Ireland

In this intimate interior Renoir depicts a fashionably dressed woman on a sofa absorbed in reading a book, perhaps a popular 'yellow-backed' novel. Her light summer hat has been cast aside and her feet, in delicate slippers, rest upon a cushion. Following the rejection of his paintings at the Salon in 1872 and 1873 Renoir forged closer links with Claude Monet and Alfred Sisley, who were soon to form the *Société Anonyme des Artistes*. During the summer of 1873 Renoir visited Monet at his Argenteuil home where he painted the artist and his family. The dark haired figure in this picture may be Monet's wife Camille, who Renoir painted reading on sofas on several occasions.[1] The woman's complexion and Spanish-style accessories also bring to mind Lise Tréhot who was Renoir's model and companion for several years until her marriage in 1872.[2] Here Renoir does not present a formal likeness of his sitter. Instead he purposely blurs the boundaries between portraiture and genre painting in order to capture the informal mood of an everyday moment.

Executed at a crucial point in Renoir's career this small modern life study draws upon a number of important artistic influences. The flurried brushwork and application of paint in thin layers gives the picture a sketchy appearance that reflects the artist's close association with Monet at this time. The dark monochrome tones, highlighted with touches of red, relate to the work of Manet, Velázquez and artists of the Spanish Golden Age. The sharp flattening of space and incorporation of chequered patterning, meanwhile, demonstrate the influence of fashionable Ukiyo-e prints by Japanese artists such as Utamaro Kitagawa.

In the last decades of the nineteenth century Impressionists such as Degas, Monet, Morisot and Caillebotte painted and sketched numerous scenes depicting men and women reclining on sofas as they read, listened to music or day-dreamed. Like Renoir's: *Young Woman in White Reading* their pictures reflect the pleasurable pursuits of a new middle class that had more time to indulge in leisure than ever before.

1 These include *Madame Claude Monet Reading* (c.1873, Sterling and Francine Clarke Institute, Williamstown, Massachusetts) and *Portrait of Madame Claude Monet* (c.1874, Museo Calouste Gulbenkian, Lisbon).

2 Compare Lise Tréhot in *Woman with Parrot* (1871, Guggenheim Museum, New York).

17. Claude Monet (1840-1926)

Interior, after Dinner, 1868/1869
Oil on canvas, 50.2 x 65.4 cm
National Gallery of Art, Washington,
Collection of Mr and Mrs Paul Mellon 1983.1.26

During the winter of 1868-69 Monet rented a house in Etretat on the Normandy coast. He stayed there for several months with his mistress Camille Doncieux and their infant son Jean hoping to evade his family's displeasure at their relationship and to avoid the expense of living in Paris. It was in the cosy dining room of this temporary home that he painted this intimate *après-diner* interior.

Monet depicts three people relaxing in front of a glowing fire. All that remains of their evening meal are coffee cups and a sugar bowl on the dining-table. Camille, in a grey dress, sits with her back to the viewer while another woman sits opposite her sewing. Camille's head is cast down like that of her companion suggesting that she too may be engaged in needlework. This other woman has not been identified but the man leaning against the fireplace is recognisable as the artist Frédéric Bazille, who was a close friend of Monet. The painting is one of two dining room scenes that Monet painted in Etretat at this time. The other painting entitled *The Dinner* (1868-69, Foundation E.G. Bührle Collection, Zurich) is larger but similar in tone and colour. It depicts Camille and Jean eating dinner with two female companions while a maid enters the scene holding a dish. Monet did not miss the busy social life of Paris and in both these Etretat pictures he depicts friends quietly enjoying each other's company by lamplight and firelight.

Throughout his career Monet was preoccupied with painting outdoors and capturing the effects of sunlight upon land and water. The dark tones and interior subject matter of this early painting contrast significantly with his luminous views of Argenteuil and Giverny painted in later years. What is intrinsic to *Interior, after Dinner*, however, and to Monet's more typically Impressionist works, is his fascination with reflected light. The centre of the composition is dominated by a hanging lamp, which shines dramatically against the shadowy backdrop of the room.[1] Its light gleams upon the scrolled frame of the lamp and falls across the tabletop, reflecting the white china on its smooth surface. At the same time the over-mantle mirror acts as a window in which one can view the reflected profiles of Bazille and the sewing woman.

[1] Bluhm and Lippincott 2000, p. 132.

18. Edgar Degas (1834-1917)
The Song Rehearsal, 1872-1873
Oil on canvas, 81 x 65 cm
Dumbarton Oaks Research Library and Collection, Washington, DC.

Ostensibly a polite drawing room scene depicting the middle-class recreational pursuit of music-making, *The Song Rehearsal* appears under closer observation to be underpinned with a fraught sense of theatricality.[1] The elegant setting is believed to be the parlour in the house of Michel Musson, Degas's uncle, on New Orleans's exclusive Esplanade. It was there that the artist stayed while in Louisiana and where his brother René lived with his wife Estelle Musson De Gas, their children and extended family.[2]

Two women appear to sing with contrived operatic gestures, accompanied by a man on piano. The woman to the left of the composition sings with open mouth and semi-closed eyes, as if emerging from the potted plant behind. She raises one hand beseechingly and presses a small book to her body with the other. The second woman holds a songbook but turns from it towards her companion's voice. The pianist also twists towards the dramatic singer; his features are indistinct, blurred, like those of a figure caught in motion in an early photograph. Degas's arrangement of the interior space disorientates and undermines visual expectations. The figures are hemmed in by a collision of furnishings and architectural details. The unadorned mass of yellow wall is anchored by the firmly scored linearity of the doorframe. Large stuffed chairs with summer slipcovers encroach upon the floor-space, echoing the forms and colouring of the women's gowns, while the polished contours of the piano merge with the man's dark clothing and features. Inanimate objects mirror the human occupants of the room and seem to collude in the domestic drama.

Intriguingly it has been suggested that the painting was influenced or inspired by the marital breakdown of René De Gas and Estelle. In 1878 he eloped to Paris with their friend and neighbour Mme Léonce Olivier. It has been argued that here, the blind Estelle (left) is interrupting a 'duet' between her husband and Mme Olivier.[3] Degas began the painting in New Orleans in 1873 and is likely to have reworked it in Paris, perhaps even after his brother's divorce (1879). It remained in his studio until his death. Like a rehearsal the painting is unresolved, a work in progress; the visible *pentimenti* and the puzzling dialogue between the figures make it a perplexing but compelling composition. Following the conventions of genre painting it invites a narrative reading but the gestures and expressions of the protagonists are strangely muted as though frozen or 'caught in the act'. The piano, traditionally a symbol of domestic harmony, is positioned towards the periphery of the parlour.[4]

1 In the late 1860s and early 1870s Degas painted several portrait groups showing people playing music within domestic settings: *M. and Mme. Edouard Manet* (c.1868-69, Singletary, fig. 4), *Lorenzo Pagans and Auguste de Gas* (c.1871-72, Musée d'Orsay, Paris) and *Violinist and Young Woman holding Sheet Music* (c.1872, The Detroit Institute of Arts).
2 Estelle Musson was Michel Musson's daughter and therefore a first cousin of her husband and Degas. Feigenbaum et al 1999, cat. 34, pp. 236-42.

3 Benfey 1997.
4 *The Song Rehearsal* like Degas's *Sulking* (c.1869-71, cat. 12) and *Interior* (c.1868-69, Philadelphia Museum of Art) frustrates interpretation. For discussions of Degas and genre see House, 'Degas's 'Tableaux de Genre'' in Kendall and Pollock, 1992, pp. 80-94 and Sidlauskus, 1993.

19. Paul Gauguin (1848-1903)

The Painter's Home, rue Carcel, 1881
Oil on canvas, 130.5 x 162.5 cm
Nasjonalgalleriet, Oslo

In the summer of 1880 Gauguin and his family moved to 8 rue Carcel, a house that they rented from the artist Félix Jobbé-Duval. It was there that Gauguin painted this large canvas, which he exhibited at the seventh Impressionist exhibition in 1882 as *Fleurs, nature morte* (*Flowers, still life*).

In the corner of a Parisian parlour a woman plays a piano, while a man leans upon it listening. These figures are largely hidden from view; the man is obscured by a folding screen and the woman by the piano. Although the couple may be modelled on the artist and his wife Mette, the painting was not intended to be viewed as a portrait. Instead, as is highlighted by the original title, Gauguin wished to emphasise the still-life aspects of the composition. Prominently displayed on the foreground table is a boldly coloured arrangement of flowers, possibly dahlia, which are tightly packed into a ceramic vase.[1] An open sketchbook and a small sewing box sit on the patterned tablecloth and beside them a ball of white thread lies like a fallen flower-head. These items suggest that the man and woman have abandoned their individual occupations to join each other at the piano. A single chair stands in the middle of the floor as if it has been just vacated. The manner in which the couple is screened off in a cosy corner of the room, beside a stove heater, emphasises the harmonious atmosphere of this domestic scene.

The modest decoration and functional appearance of the room are appropriate for a newly rented house. However, the residents appear to have created a sense of homeliness with decorative details such as the screen, tablecloth, ceramic figurine and the wooden clogs and rug that hang on the wall. These items not only denote the couple's personal tastes and interests but also hint at Gauguin's future preoccupations with Breton subjects, craft and Japanese art. With the exception of the floral display, Gauguin has not greatly differentiated between the status of the objects and occupants within his interior. He has painted this domestic still-life with a series of feathery brushstrokes that melt and merge in undulating tones. It is as if the piano's music and the flowers' scent have temporarily coloured the reality of the room.

[1] Gauguin may have been aware of the Symbolist poet
Paul Verlaine's poem 'Un Dahlia', *Poèmes saturniens* (1866).

20. Mary Cassatt (1844-1926)

Lydia at a Tapestry Frame, c.1881

Oil on canvas, 65 x 92 cm

Collection of the Flint Institute of Arts, Flint, Michigan

The American artist Mary Cassatt settled in Paris in 1874, the year of the first Impressionist exhibition. She initially exhibited at the Salon and was disheartened when her works were rejected by the jury in 1877. Following this she became associated with the Impressionists and on the invitation of Degas exhibited with the group four times from 1879. Despite being a woman *and* a foreigner Cassatt was accepted into the male-dominated art world with exceptional ease. Inspired by her deep admiration for Degas's work she focused on familiar domestic subjects rather than landscapes or exterior scenes of city life.

Following the relocation of her parents and sister to Paris in 1877, the day-to-day activities of Cassatt's family soon came to dominate the subjects of her paintings, pastels and prints. Social circumstances dictated that nineteenth-century women spent most of their time at home and Cassatt reflects this through her depictions of women and children reading, drinking tea and conversing.

Just as her friend Berthe Morisot used her sister Edma as a model, Cassatt relied on her older sister Lydia (1837-82). Lydia suffered from Bright's disease, a chronic kidney condition, from which she died in 1882. In the final years of her life she was increasingly confined to home where Cassatt devotedly kept her company painting, and Lydia herself passed the time reading or engaged in needlework. In this painting Lydia is depicted at a close angle as she works on a tapestry. Her location by the window provides both sisters with sufficient daylight in which to carry out their artistic endeavours.

Cassatt's Impressionism is evident in her treatment of reflected light and sketchy brushwork. This sketchiness and the unpainted edges of the canvas might have been prompted by Lydia's inability to sit for long periods at this time. The 'bamboo' tapestry frame and Cassatt's use of calligraphic strokes of black paint convey an interest in Japanese art that would strongly influence her prints in the 1890s.

21. Berthe Morisot (1841-1895)

The Artist's Sister at a Window, 1869

Oil on canvas, 54.8 x 46.3 cm

National Gallery of Art, Washington,

Ailsa Mellon Bruce Collection 1970.14.47

Berthe Morisot exhibited this intimate study of her older sister Edma at the Salon of 1870, four years prior to the first Impressionist exhibition. It anticipates the inside-outside motifs of balconies, windows, doorways and conservatories which feature repeatedly in the work of Caillebotte, Degas and Monet.

In March 1869 Edma married a naval officer, Adolphe Pontillon, and moved to the sea-port town of Lorient in Brittany. Much to their distress it was the first time that the sisters had lived apart and Morisot painted this work during that summer, when she visited the newlyweds at Lorient. Prior to painting this work Morisot had focused on *plein- air* scenes for which Edma occasionally modelled. The sisters' retreat into a domestic interior space may have been prompted by the summer heat or perhaps by a new sense of propriety following Edma's marriage. Before she married, Edma, like her sister was an aspiring artist and had exhibited at the Salon in 1864, 1865, 1867 and 1868. In this intimate portrait her chair faces the balcony but Edma, rather than enjoying the view, gazes downwards at a decorated fan. In the company of her artist-sister she seems contemplative, resigned to her new roles as wife and as subject, not creator of art. Her own stillness and the trellis pattern on the drawing room wallpaper reinforce the sense that she is held in a fragile 'gilded cage'.

In her depiction of this shady interior, Morisot pays special attention to the natural light that floods through the open *porte-fenêtre* and highlights Edma's full white gown with accents of pink and lilac. Entitling her portrait *Jeune femme à sa fenêtre* (*Young woman at her window*) when it was exhibited at the Salon,[1] Morisot may have been inspired by James McNeil Whistler's innovative paintings of women in white.[2] Her depiction of the 'jeune femme' does not simply portray a woman in an elegant interior but is a study of *interiority* by one intimately in tune with the sitter. This presentation of the newly married Mme Pontillon is an exploration of light, colour and contemplation.

---

1 Morisot also exhibited *The Mother and Sister of the Artist* (1869/70).

2 See Whistler's *Symphony in White, No. 1: The White Girl* (1862, National Gallery of Art, Washington), which was shown at the Salon des Refusés in 1863 as *Dame blanche*.

22. Edouard Manet (1832-1883)

Interior at Arcachon, 1871
Oil on canvas, 39.4 x 53.7 cm
Sterling and Francine Clark Art Institute,
Williamstown, Massachusetts, USA

The Franco-Prussian War (1870-71) deeply undermined Parisian family life even for those from affluent backgrounds, such as Edouard Manet.[1] In September 1870 Manet sent his wife Suzanne and eighteen-year-old stepson Léon Koëlla-Leenhoff out of the besieged city to Oloron-Sainte-Marie in the French Pyrenees. He joined them the following February, staying briefly at Bordeaux before moving to Arcachon, Le Pouliguen and Tours before returning to Paris in May, after the fall of the Commune.

Manet painted this interior scene at the Chalet Servantie, a seaside villa that the family occupied for the month of March.[2] Mme Manet is seated at the left of the composition, her back to the viewer, and looking towards the sea. A rotund and rather matronly figure, she occupies a high-backed seat and props a red stockinged foot upon a folding stool. Her crossed leg forms an impromptu table on which she balances the pages of a journal or letter. On the right, Mme Manet's son sits sideways at a table; he holds a pen to his mouth and rests an open book on his lap. His hair is dishevelled, perhaps from sea-breezes, and his upturned boater sits on a chair behind. Dominating the centre of this interior is an almost abstract exterior space; a tripartite layering of sand, sea and sky.[3] In contemporaneous genre painting this open space or 'missing' wall would be the likely location of a hearth; the nucleus for a narrative and welcoming focal point of the home. Manet however had no interest in painting anecdotal fireside scenes and here divides the room, allowing light and air to filter in and creating a picture within the picture.

The room is modestly decorated and clear of the pictures, clutter and collectable objects common in the 1870s Parisian bourgeois home.[4] Although it is a temporary abode, the location of an enforced vacation, the atmosphere is not unpleasant.[5] It could even be argued that the family has embraced its make-do surroundings. Suzanne sits in the more homely area, which features a clock, gilded mirror and rug. The youthful Léon by contrast sits on a stool, bare boards beneath his feet, musing in the manner of a bohemian poet.[6] Manet, the unseen 'paterfamilias' is, we imagine, positioned directly in line with the open doors – reflecting his longstanding love of the sea. In this transitional 'home' the displaced family members write, paint and contemplate – it is, in a sense, a dream interior.

1 See Clayson 2002.
2 41 Avenue Ste Marie, Arcachon.
3 A related drawing presents a more detailed exterior view and gives greater prominence to the figure of Léon; *Mme. Manet and her Son at Arcachon* (1871, Fogg Art Museum, Harvard)
4 Compare for example, Zacharie Astruc's, *Parisian Interior* (1874, Musée d'Evreux, cat. 13).

5 Manet's Arcachon existence was more modest than usual but not unhappy. In a letter to Théodore Duret from the Chalet Servanti (6 March 1871) he asked for money and said 'we were very sorry not to see you at Arcachon, you could have spent a pleasant day here', quoted in Wilson-Bareau 2004, p. 114.
6 Compare for example Gustave Courbet, *Portrait of Baudelaire* (c.1848, Musée Fabre, Montpellier) and Manet's later *Portrait of Stéphane Mallarmé* (1876, Musée d'Orsay, Paris).

23. Berthe Morisot (1841-1895)

Eugène Manet on the Isle of Wight, 1875

Oil on canvas, 38 x 46 cm

Musée Marmottan Monet, Paris

In December 1874, Berthe Morisot married Eugène Manet, an amateur painter and novelist and the brother of Edouard Manet. The following summer the couple holidayed on the Isle of Wight and in London. It was during their stay at Cowes that Morisot painted this portrait, in which she depicts her husband sitting by a window in their boarding house overlooking the harbour from Queen's Parade.[1]

Although veiled and fragmented by the curtains and dissecting bars of the window frame, the composition comprises mostly sky, sea and garden. Eugène appears uncomfortably confined, and the chair, geraniums and garden fence-posts form a series of 'obstacles' hemming him indoors. His line of vision coincides with a strip of open space, which partially reveals the fleeting figures of a girl and a nursemaid. Morisot wrote to her sister Edma from Cowes complaining that bad weather and her poor command of English had made painting *en plein air* problematic. She continued:

> People come and go on the jetty, and it is impossible to catch them. It is the same with the boats. There is extraordinary life and movement but how is one to render it? I began something in the sitting room, of Eugène. The poor man has taken your place [as a sitter]. But he is a less obliging model: at once it becomes too much for him.[2]

While Morisot frequently posed for her brother-in-law Edouard Manet, it was relatively unorthodox for a female artist to paint her husband. Eugène was deeply supportive of his new wife's career but here he appears somewhat 'on edge'. In a letter home she admitted: 'Cowes is very pretty but not gay; besides we constantly miss our home life. Eugène is even more uncommunicative than I'.[3] Morisot has painted this hotel room interior with the sketchy immediacy and the vibrant colouring characteristic of her landscapes. Her focus on the exterior view and her husband's restlessness reinforce the couple's mutual desire to be in the sea air.[4]

1 Morisot exhibited watercolours from her Isle of Wight stay at the 1875 Impressionist exhibition. This work was first exhibited at the Durand–Ruel Gallery in 1896 as *En Angleterre*.

2 Morisot 1986, p. 101.

3 Morisot 1986, p. 102.

4 In subsequent portraits Eugène is depicted in garden scenes.

24. Edgar Degas (1834-1917)

Yard of a House (New Orleans, Study), 1872-1873

Oil on canvas, 60 x 75 cm

Ordrupgaard, Copenhagen

This New Orleans scene depicts several of Degas's nieces and nephews at the threshold of their grandfather's home on the Esplanade.[1] Painted from within, the children and their nursemaid congregate around the back door, which leads onto a garden path and a gate opening onto the street. Like *Portraits in a Cotton Office (New Orleans)*, (1873, cat. 10), the composition is built upon geometric structures and a series of layered openings into partially revealed views. In both pictures a vertical door jamb acts as a framing device. Here the sash window on the left is part-opened but a green shutter obstructs the view. This painting is engagingly contradictory: it is both an interior and an exterior, a portrait and a genre scene, sketchy and unresolved but signed and varnished.[2] It was one of twenty-four works that Degas exhibited at the second Impressionist exhibition (1876), where it was catalogued as *Cour d'une maison (Nouvelle-Orléans. Esquisse)*.

As well as fulfilling Degas's fascination with sophisticated framing devices and the juxtaposition of the public and private worlds of street and home, there were practical reasons why he positioned the children in this in-between space. By the early 1870s his eyesight had started to deteriorate, a condition exacerbated by the bright sunlight of New Orleans. The choice of indoor or semi-indoor subjects was determined by Degas's intense fear of inflicting further damage. He wrote to Henri Rouart:

> The light is so strong that I have not yet been able to do anything on the river. My eyes are so greatly in need of care that I scarcely take any risk with them at all. A few family portraits will be the sum total of my efforts, I was unable to avoid that and assuredly would not wish to complain if it were less difficult, if the settings were less insipid and the models less restless.[3]

A few months later he conceded that he managed to keep his eyes 'sufficiently half open to see my fill.'[4] This threshold scene is 'half open' to the outside world; a compromise between the children's wish to play outdoors and their artist-uncle's inability to venture to the garden. It would seem that the (unseen) artist, nursemaid, mastiff and standing girl gently corral the three younger infants towards the doorstep, so that their impression can be captured quickly before they are released into the sunshine.

1 John Rewald identifies the porch as that of a house on the Millaudon plantation fifteen miles outside New Orleans, which was owned by friends of the Musson family: 'Degas and his family in New Orleans' in Rewald, 1985, pp. 26-46. For a detailed discussion on the identities of the children see Feigenbaum et al, 1999.

2 Birgitte Anderberg argues that Degas's sketchy technique relates to state of the children's 'unfinished' state of development. Lederballe and Rabinow, 2002, pp. 111-13
3 Letter from Degas to Henri Rouart, 5 December, 1872. Degas, 1947, p. 25.
4 Letter from Degas to James Tissot, 18 February 1873. Degas, 1947, p. 31.

25. Paul Gauguin (1848-1903)

The Little Dreamer, 1881

Oil on canvas, 60 x 74 cm

Ordrupgaard, Copenhagen

Gauguin exhibited this painting at the seventh Impressionist exhibition (1882) where it was catalogued as *La Petite rêve. Etude*. The artist's only daughter Aline (b.1877) is depicted sleeping in a wrought iron day-bed.[1] Her bare legs, light gown and lack of coverings suggest her rest is a siesta rather than a night-time sleep; a folded blanket is sandwiched between her feet and another, rumpled, is pushed to one side. The bed's foliated scrollwork combine with the cool green tones of the wallpaper to convey a sense of alfresco repose. The wallpaper is exquisitely decorated with fan-shaped ginkgo leaves and silhouetted birds; to the left a bird perches on a nest overlooking its young, at the centre another is in flight. On the wallpaper's edge above the child's head runs a half-hidden line of musical notation, suggesting a soothing birdsong lullaby. This drifting tune enhances the notion that the child is being transported into a dreamlike state on her *lit-bateau*.

Dangling from the bed is a jester doll who wears a colourful costume that includes a striped hat and jerkin edged with tiny bells. The beard and facial features of this clownish mascot resemble those of Gauguin himself and perhaps playfully connote the mascot's role as a symbolic father-figure or protector. Gauguin later used the emblems of 'sleeper' and 'watcher' to more sinister effect in his Tahitian painting *Manao tupapau* (*The Spirit of the Dead Watching*) (1892, Albright-Knox Art Gallery, Buffalo, New York), in which a Polynesian girl lies wide-eyed and fearfully conscious that the ghostly spectre of a Tupapau (spirit) stands by her bedside.[2]

The Little Dreamer was most likely painted at Gauguin's home in the rue Carcel (see cat. 19). During the years that he lived there he frequently looked to his domestic environment for subjects and to his children for sitters.[3] *The Little Dreamer* is an interior painting in a dual sense; it depicts the interior of the child's room but it also alludes to her dream-interior. Gauguin's addition of the word '*étude*' (study) to the title of this technically finished picture is purposefully suggestive. The word's musical resonances reinforce the idea that the composition is an *impression*, as much about mood as material realities. With its allusions to dreams, musicality, interiority, the child-state and natural world, this 'everyday' domestic scene anticipates with an understated intensity Gauguin's Symbolism.

1 Lederballe and Rabinow (2002), cat. 55, pp. 188-90.
2 Claire Frèches Thory in Brettel et al 1988, cat. 154, pp. 279-82.

3 This picture relates closely to *Sleeping Child* (1884, private collection) in which a girl rests her head upon a table before a similar Japanoise wallpaper.

26. Federico Zandomeneghi (1841-1917)

In Bed, 1878

Oil on canvas, 60 x 74 cm

Galleria d'Arte Moderna, Palazzo Pitti, Florence

From 1862 to 1866 the Venetian-born painter Federico Zandomeneghi lived in Florence where he became involved with the *Macchiaioli* group. During this time he formed a friendship with the influential art-critic Diego Martelli that was to become an important influence on his subsequent career.[1] In 1874 Zandomeneghi moved to Paris, perhaps prompted by Martelli's enthusiastic reports of the first Impressionist exhibition which he had seen at the Boulevard des Capucines. Before long he became acquainted with artists from avant-garde circles who frequented the Café de la Nouvelle-Athènes including Renoir, Manet, fellow Italian Giuseppe de Nittis and most importantly Degas. Through Degas's invitation Zandomeneghi exhibited at the Impressionist exhibitions of 1879, 1880, 1881 and 1886. He stayed independent from the group but maintained a fervent admiration for Degas, drawing inspiration from his late pastels and on occasion copying from his work.[2]

In Bed (A Letto) encapsulates the motifs of rest, repose and leisure that were key sources of inspiration to artists in Impressionists circles. Zandomeneghi shows a young girl reclining in bed, her head resting upon her arm which in turn lies upon a pillow and bolster. Long strands of auburn hair fall across the pillow and like the tousled white sheets which reveal her torso are arranged with artful abandon. The blue eiderdown is painted with Impressionistic dashes of colour, adding light, contrast and texture to its floral fabric. In the corner of the room a gilded bar divides the elaborate wallpaper which is decorated with an abstracted print of twisting leaves and lily-like blossoms. The shimmering intricacy of the wall decoration, the heavy wooden headboard and the comfortably upholstered bed suggest a sophisticated Parisian interior. An almost identical 'gilded corner' is the setting for Gustave Caillebotte's *Young Man at the Piano* (1876, Singletary, fig. 6). Indeed an echo of Caillebotte's refined realism pervades *In Bed*.

Zandomeneghi has appropriated elements of Impressionism: painting in a fresh white light, using softly contrasting and sketchy brushwork, and choosing an intimately informal subject matter. Despite these factors, a mood of classical restraint underpins the painting. Zandomeneghi has balanced his composition to present the girl in the tranquil corner of a boudoir, rather than in a randomly cropped and cluttered one as Degas might have done.

1 Zandomeneghi and Degas exhibited portraits of Martelli at the fourth Impressionist exhibition (1879); Zandomeneghi depicted him seated in an armchair before a fireplace (Galleria d'Arte Moderna, Florence) while Degas portrayed him at a paper strewn desk in a study (National Gallery of Scotland, Edinburgh).
2 Ann Dumas 2003.

27. Federico Zandomeneghi (1841-1917)

The awakening, 1895

Pastel on card, 60 x 73 cm

Collezione Mondadori, Museo Civico Palazzo Te, Mantova, Italy

This intensely-coloured pastel depicts a woman from behind seated on an upholstered arm-chair. Turning her face to the side she extends her arms above her head, with fingers intertwined. Her loosely bound hair, white chemise and silk slippers indicate that it is morning. Behind the chair rests the patterned fabric of an abandoned dressing-gown or shawl which may have just fallen from her hands. In the background, a uniformed maid bends forward into an armoire to select her mistress's clothing for the day. The faces of both women are hidden from view. The indulgent pose of the mistress befits her comfortable surroundings: the floor is covered with a red carpet, to the right a brilliant blue curtain conceals a still-warm bed while to the left a dresser holds a gilded mirror and decorative ornaments.

The awakening (*Il risveglio*) was executed some twenty-one years after Zandomeneghi's arrival in Paris in 1874, the year of the first Impressionist exhibition. It demonstrates how his subject matter and technique continued to be deeply informed by the work of Degas long after the final Impressionist exhibition of 1886. Several elements of this composition are directly attributable to Degas's influence. Zandomeneghi partially conceals his figures but rather than cropping them in the Japanese manner like Degas, he uses elements within the setting such as the wardrobe door and mistress's sleeve as masking devices. The mass of red hair, silver bangle and nightgown are details which feature repeatedly in Degas's works. However the woman's feline stretch is far removed from the coarse vulgarity that critics perceived in pastel nudes that Degas exhibited in 1886.[1] Indeed *The awakening* appears conservative when compared with Degas's contemporaneous *After the Bath* (c.1896, cat. 34), with its contorted figure, restricted palette and dramatic shadows. Both Degas and Zandomeneghi found subjects in the intimate privacy of the female boudoir but whereas Degas located his scenes in interiors across the social spectrum, Zandomeneghi's are undeniably bourgeois.

In this late work Zandomeneghi uses vivid strand-like strokes of contrasting colour to convey the light of this morning scene. Multiple individualised touches allow the contours of figures and furnishings to dissolve, merge, and melt into each other. This play of form and colour relates to the artist's growing interest in Italian Divisionism and French Neo-Impressionism.

1 Degas's group of pastels was titled *Suite de nuds [sic] de femmes se baignant, se lavant, se séchant, s'essuyant, se poignant ou se faisant peigne.*

28. Childe Hassam (1859-1935)

The French Breakfast, 1910
Oil on canvas, 73 x 50.2 cm
Collection Carmen Thyssen-Bornemisza
on loan to the Museo Thyssen-Bornemisza

In June 1910 the Boston-born artist Childe Hassam travelled to Europe for the fourth time, painting and visiting museums in London, the Netherlands, Spain and France. He arrived in Paris in mid-July, where he and his wife Maude spent three weeks. The couple stayed at the Hôtel de l'Empire on the rue Daunou where Maude modelled for this informal interior. Entitled *The French Breakfast* the scene was not intended as a portrait but rather as a portrayal of leisurely life in the manner of Berthe Morisot and Hassam's compatriot Mary Cassatt.[1]

Cocooned in her canopied bed the woman looks down upon a breakfast tray that bears, among many other items a coffee pot, a milk jug and a salt cellar. Red curtains fall from ceiling to floor to frame the performance of the breakfast and add a theatrical flourish to the composition. A pair of slippers rest by the bed, while a dressing gown and fringed shawl lie across a chair in preparation for the woman's rising. The room is decorated with many of the trappings of a European bourgeois apartment: carved furniture, a gilded mirror, white linen and lace, a chinoiserie jug and basin and richly patterned wall coverings. On the bedside wall however, a service bell with an accompanying notice indicates that this is a hotel room rather than a domestic interior. Like Manet's *Interior at Arcachon* (1871, cat. 22) and Morisot's *Eugène Manet on the Isle of Wight* (1875, cat. 23), Hassam's picture portrays the artist's spouse in a 'home from home' environment.

From Paris Hassam wrote to his friend J. Alden Weir complaining that the city was noisy, dirty and 'all torn up like New York' with building work.[2] Perhaps this is why all three of the pictures he is known to have painted during his stay were executed at the Hôtel de l'Empire. *July Fourteenth, rue Daunou* (1910, Metropolitan Museum of Art, New York) records a flag-fringed street from the high viewpoint of the hotel balcony, while *At the Writing Desk* (1910, Private Collection) is set in the corner of a room before tall French-doors. Outside a French tricolour can be seen hanging from the building. Appropriately, Hassam painted each of these Parisian scenes in a highly 'Impressionist' manner, emphasising light and textural variations with colourful 'criss-crossing' brushstrokes and bold touches of pure pigment.

1 Hassam may have been aware of Morisot's *Le Lever* (1886, Private Collection), exhibited at the 1886 Impressionist exhibition a few months before he visited Paris for the first time. Kenneth W. Maddox suggests that Hassam's composition may have been inspired by Jan van Eyck's *The Arnolfini Portrait* (1434, National Gallery London) which he may have seen in London prior to arriving in Paris. Information provided by Museo Thyssen-Bornemisza.

2 Letter from Hassam to Weir, 21 July 1910, quoted in Weinberg et al 2004, pp. 189-91.

29. Edgar Degas (1834-1917)

The Convalescent, c.1872-1887
Oil on canvas, 65.1 x 47 cm
The J. Paul Getty Museum, Los Angeles

The identity of the woman in *The Convalescent* has been the subject of much debate, as have when and where the picture was executed.[1] What is documented is that the art dealer Durand-Ruel purchased the painting from Degas on 31 January 1887 as *La malade*.

Wearing a shapeless white shift and enveloped in a dark dressing gown the invalid's weighty form occupies most of the canvas. Behind her we see the suggested shape of an unmade bed and some loosely patterned wallpaper. Leaning a heavy head upon her hand the young woman seems pensive, her eyes red and sore.[2] By omitting extraneous details, such as furnishings, cups, plates, tea trays and the clutter of everyday domesticity, Degas presents a 'poetic' rather than a particularised interior space.[3] The pyramidic prominence of the convalescent powerfully conveys the enforced ennui and oppressive claustrophobia of the sickroom. Degas's images of modern life are usually populated by women and provide glimpses into the private spaces of dressing and rehearsal rooms, boudoirs and millineries. This interior scene is intensely intimate - the woman is positioned so close to the picture plane that we seem to observe her through a keyhole.

Through his friendship with James Tissot, Degas became interested in contemporary English painting. The languid pose and tearful expression of his convalescent call to mind William Holman Hunt's painting *Isabella and the Pot of Basil* (1867, Laing Art Gallery, Newcastle upon Tyne), as does the empty white bed. Like Hunt, Degas underpins his scene with a melancholic mood, though sets it firmly in the modern-day and not in the nostalgic romance of literature or history. The subject of convalescence was not uncommon in nineteenth-century art. Degas painted several images associated with the subject of illness including *Woman with Bandage* (1872-73, The Detroit Institute of Art), *The Nurse* (1872-73, Private Collection) and *Young Woman seated in a Garden* (c.1868-73, Private Collection). Their association with the home and with an ideal of tragic beauty meant that women were typically the convalescents of choice for artists. However, on occasion men became the subjects of sickroom paintings such as the bed-bound Claude Monet in Frédéric Bazille's *L'ambulance improvisée* (1865, Musée d'Orsay, Paris).

1 It has been proposed that the model for this picture may have been one of Degas's cousins, Désirée or Estelle Musson. For an overview of this debate see Boggs in Feigenbaum et al 1999, pp. 191-92.

2 See Marni Kessler, 'Ocular Anxiety and the Pink Tea Cup: Edgar Degas's *Woman with Bandage*', *Nineteenth-Century Art Worldwide*, 5:2 (Fall 2006).

3 Degas's painting *Melancholy* (1874, Phillips Collection, Washington, DC) similarly presents a despondent woman ensconced within a domestic interior; her body and clothing seem to merge into the chaise longue on which she sits.

30. Edgar Degas (1834-1917)

Woman at her Toilet, c.1894
Charcoal and pastel on paper, 95.6 x 109.9 cm
Tate: Presented by C. Frank Stoop, 1933

Second only to the working lives of ballet dancers, depictions of the daily rituals of the female toilette make up a large proportion of Degas's *oeuvre*. Among these images of women bathing and dressing are around thirty pictures of women brushing or combing their hair. Here a seated woman wearing a loose shift or nightgown pulls a comb through a thick mass of auburn locks. Holding her left hand to the side of her head she appears to push against it to make the hair taut.

The woman occupies a shallow space, perhaps the corner of a bedroom. A maid enters the scene from the side, stirring a breakfast cup of tea or coffee. Her head is cropped by the picture frame and her lower body hidden by the dressing table. A vase, decorated in oriental blue and white, partially overlaps her body. Both the decorative vase and the attentive maid have curved profiles; cut-off and still, they play ancillary roles in the scene. The background, by contrast, is alive, animated by an unravelling, lively wallpaper pattern which is vibrantly coloured in clashing tones of yellow, green, blue and pink. The vivid blue fabric of what appears to be a dressing gown hangs from the wall like an impromptu curtain.

Another of Degas's women combing her hair has been compared to a musician. With cupped hand to her ear she is said to comb her hair 'as if the comb were a bow.'[1] This musical analogy can be taken further in *Woman at her Toilet*. Here, it seems as though the seated woman plays a cello, her hair forming the strings of the invisible instrument. Green and rust-toned lines emanate from her body. It is as if they are the manifestation of vibrating sound tremors filtering into the interior and temporarily transforming the atmospheric tone and colour of the room. This merging of a female figure with her physical environment anticipates Edouard Vuillard's densely patterned interiors of the 1890s, in which the figurative elements are absorbed into the furnishings.

1 Boggs description of *Young Woman combing her Hair*, (c.1890-92, Musée d'Orsay, Paris) in Boggs et al 1988, cat 310, p. 517.

31. Edgar Degas (1834-1917)

Femme se coiffant, c.1884

Oil on canvas, 61 x 74 cm

Private Collection, courtesy of Pyms Gallery, London

The title of this painting and a related study in the Courtauld Institute of Art suggest that the scene depicts a woman arranging her hair.[1] It is however more likely that both pictures belong to the series of works centred on the subject of milliners' shops, which Degas executed between c.1882-86. Here an elegant woman, silhouetted like a black-swan, sits with her back to the viewer. Looking towards the white gleam of a mirror she raises both hands to the back of her head to adjust a small hat.[2] The setting is unspecified but the broad band of skirting and the neutral vertical bands of the wallpaper (or perhaps a muslin-curtained window) are elements familiar to other millinery shop scenes by Degas. The deep chair on which the woman perches is not designed for relaxation but is a temporary site for posing. The red carpet enlivens and enriches the interior space. In combination with the muted blacks, browns and greys it lends an Old Master quality to this deliberately casual glimpse of everyday life.

The woman's neat dark jacket and swathe of skirt form the costume of an urbane bourgeois woman. The curved outline of her back is reminiscent of Degas's depictions of Mary Cassatt exploring the Paintings and Etruscan Galleries of the Louvre (1879-80). Indeed the model for *Femme se coiffant* may have been Cassatt, who is known to have posed as a customer in two milliner's shop scenes and who admitted to sitting for Degas 'once in a while when he finds the movement difficult, and the model cannot seem to get his idea'.[3] As in so many of his female-focused interiors Degas shows the woman from behind, corroborating his friend Edmond Duranty's statement that 'a back should reveal temperament, age and social position.'[4] This interior scene represents a private viewing in a semi-public space. In the nineteenth century Parisian millinery shops were the preserve of wealthy women. They offered an intimate shopping experience behind closed doors, where customers could enjoy fittings and consultations away from the glare of the shop window and floor. Degas occasionally visited millinery shops with female friends and gained a privileged insight into their exclusive rituals. Here, his broad outlining of the woman's form and use of warm dark strokes of colour heighten the enigmatic atmosphere of the interior.

1 *Femme assise se coiffant*, c.1884, charcoal, chalk, pastel on paper, 63 x 76 cm, The Samuel Courtauld Trust, Courtauld Institute of Art Gallery, London.

2 Degas used the same triangular arrangement of arms, with head at the apex, for the customer in *At the Milliner's*, (1882, pastel on paper, Museo Thyssen-Bornemisza, Madrid).

3 Mary Cassatt quoted in Havemeyer 1961, p. 258. Cassatt sat for the pastels: *At the Milliner's* (c.1882, Museum of Modern Art, New York) and *At the Milliner's* (1882, Metropolitan Museum of Art, New York).

4 Duranty (1876) in Moffett et al 1986, pp. 477-84.

32. Berthe Morisot (1841-1895)

Le Corsage Noir, 1878
Oil on canvas, 73 x 65 cm
National Gallery of Ireland

Between 1878 and 1880, Berthe Morisot painted several portrait-style compositions, which presented fashionably dressed women positioned in front of loosely painted backgrounds. Each of these works was designed as a vehicle for exploring light and colour.

Le Corsage Noir is a study in black. It presents a woman (posed by a professional model) dressed for an evening at the theatre. She wears a black gown with a close fitting bodice that belonged to the artist and which Morisot had worn in formal studio photographs in 1875. Her hair is loosely dressed and she is accessorised with a jet choker, gold earrings, a stole and gloves. The painting was executed in the artist's studio but the imaginary setting it depicts is purposefully indistinct. The vertical line extending above the woman's shoulder implies that she may sit in the corner of a fashionable drawing room. Her chair's gilded armrest conveys a sense of comfortable luxury. To the right-hand side of the composition, green foliage extends behind the woman's shoulder and acts as a lively framing device.

This work relates closely to *Young Woman dressed for the Ball* (1879, Musée d'Orsay, Paris), which was simply titled *Portrait* when first exhibited in 1880. Whereas *Le Corsage Noir* depicts a woman in black, this slightly later picture shows a woman wearing a pale pink-white gown, before a lightly coloured floral background. In turn, this 'pair' of evening pictures, can be related to the artist's daytime depictions of fashionable women, *Summer* (c.1878, Musée Fabre, Montpelier) and *Winter* (1878-80, Dallas Museum of Art) both of which are also painterly exercises in colour.

Morisot painted this 'imagined interior' in 1878. Her daughter Julie was born in November that year. In the months surrounding Julie's birth Morisot could not paint outdoors with the freedom that she had previously enjoyed. It may have been these circumstances that prompted her to explore the effects of light and colour within the studio rather than *en plein air*.

Le Corsage Noir is depicted hanging in the background of Morisot's domestic interior *La Coiffure* (1894, Museo Nacional de Bella Artes, Buenos Aires). It remained in the possession of the artist's daughter until 1936.

33. Paul Gauguin (1848-1903)

Nude study (*Woman sewing*), 1880

Oil on canvas, 114.5 x 79.5 cm

Ny Carlsberg Glyptotek, Copenhagen

Gauguin exhibited this bedroom interior at the sixth Impressionist exhibition in 1881 giving it the title *Etude de Nu* (*Nude Study*). The painting portrays a nude woman sewing as she sits on an unmade bed. It would appear as though she is mending undergarments before dressing. The woman's body dominates the centre of the composition with a lumpy solidity. Gauguin has not retouched his model's skin with an Academic 'airbrush' but has painted it with feathery fragmented brushstrokes, rendering it mottled in colour and uneven in texture.

The scene is staged in a shallow, compacted space close to the picture plane. Hanging on the pale purple wall behind the figure is a woven rug and a mandolin, details that suggest a bohemian rather than a bourgeois setting.[1] Gauguin included the emblem of the mandolin in several still-life compositions including *Mandolin on a Chair* (1880, Private Collection) and *Dahlias and Mandolin* (1883, Private Collection). The addition of this instrument, which is typically associated with seventeenth-century Dutch painting, highlights the artist's desire to reinvent pictorial Realism for modern subjects. The woman's sculptural form makes her an integral element in what is essentially a nude still-life study.

Gauguin's picture disturbed the public and most critics who attended the 1881 exhibition. They found his model physically unattractive and his naturalistic portrayal of her nudity vulgar. One of the few critics to praise the picture was Joris-Karl Huysmans who likened the figure's fleshy realism to Rembrandt's nudes. He proclaimed 'she is a modern girl and not a girl posing for an exhibition, she is neither lascivious nor simpering, she is quite simply darning her clothes.'[2] Mary Cassatt and Camille Pissarro also showed pictures of modern women engaged in needlework at the exhibition and, like Gauguin, painted their models with an emphasis on naturalism.[3] Gauguin's sewing woman, though influenced by Dutch Old Masters and Ingres's *Valpinçon Bather* (1808, Musée du Louvre), upset contemporary critics as she was nude and located in an undistinguished contemporary interior.

[1] The edge of this or a similar rug appears in *The Painter's Home, rue Carcel* (1881, cat. 19). Richard Brettell notes that this work was likely to have been set in Impasse Frémin before Gauguin moved to rue Carcel in October 1880.

[2] Huysmans, *L'Art moderne* (1883), Harrison, Paul Wood and Jason Gaiger, 1998, p. 892.

[3] Camille Pissarro *La Ravaudeuse* (1881, location unknown), Mary Cassatt, Le Jardin [*Lydia Crocheting in the Garden at Marly*] (1880, The Metropolitan Museum of Art, New York).

34. Edgar Degas (1834-1917)

After the Bath (Woman drying herself), c.1896
Oil on canvas, 89.5 x 116.8 cm
Philadelphia Museum of Art:
Purchased with funds from the estate of George D. Widener, 1980

In 1886 Degas exhibited a group of female nudes in pastel at the final Impressionist exhibition. These works depicted women variously engaged in their toilette; washing backs, towelling toes dry and arranging hair. Composed as if they gave glimpses into the women's everyday lives, these drawings showed them in awkward but convincing poses.

After the Bath (Woman drying herself) is one of three related oil paintings of bathers that Degas executed around 1896.[1] In this, the most dramatic of the group, he realises the scene with an intensity of form and colouring that marks a move away from naturalism and towards abstraction.

A woman kneels on a chaise longue and dries her body while leaning against its upholstered back-rest. This piece of furniture is not used for comfort but instead acts as a staging device, with which Degas elevates and arranges his model to impressive pictorial effect.[2] At the opposite side of the room sits a vacated bath-tub, which has been cropped to leave just one elliptical edge. In this painting Degas has eliminated extraneous detail and avoided a detailed description of the interior. His use of colouring is also minimal. The wall, floor, sofa, bath and woman's head are all described in deeply saturated red tones. Degas delineated the contours of forms in black, but used white to highlight the woman's body and the towel that acts as a 'backdrop'.

Degas affords his bather a contorted elegance that is posed rather than random. A related drawing (Private Collection) and photograph (The J. Paul Getty Museum, Los Angeles), indicate that this sparse boudoir interior was 'stage-set' by Degas.

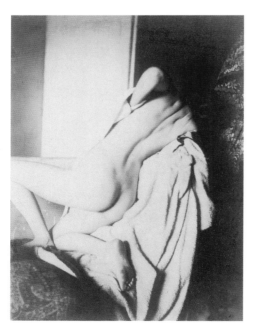

Edgar Degas, *After the Bath, Woman Drying Her Back*, 1896
Gelatin silver, 16.5 x 12cm.
The J. Paul Getty Museum, Los Angeles

1 The other paintings are in private collections. Boggs et al 1988, pp. 548-52
2 Degas frequently used chairs as propping devices for his models, see cats. 6 and 7.

35. Pierre Bonnard (1867-1947)

Grandmother and Child, 1894

Oil on panel, 34.4 x 41.9 cm

Leeds Museums and Galleries

Domestic interiors were a constant source of inspiration to Bonnard, whose work is described as *intimisme* in style. Typically, Bonnard depicted family members at mealtimes and often would paint several versions of the same scene with slight variations in the poses and place settings. Among Bonnard's sitters were his maternal grandmother Mme Frédéric Mertzdorff and his mother Elizabeth Mertzdoff. These women were often shown attending to their grandchildren, cutting food, spoon feeding or supervising.

These small paintings on board are intimate studies of the artist's mother and his sister's first child Jean (b.1892). *Grandmother and Child* (cat. 35) was painted in 1894 and *Boy eating Cherries* (cat. 36) in the summer of 1895. The development of the child in this year is notable. In the earlier work he sits with a napkin tied under his chin while his grandmother feeds him from a dish. In the 1895 picture his chequered shirt is uncovered and he eats cherries, which are spread upon a white tablecloth, while his grandmother keeps watch. This contrast of age and youth is poignantly reinforced as Jean has more hair in the later picture while his grandmother's hair is a little more grey.

The pictures are painted from the same angle. They focus on the table and the figure of the child, both of which are 'framed' by the grandmother's body. Despite this, the colouring and technique employed in each scene are quite different. The 1894 picture is more muted in tone and the paint is thinly applied. Here the grandmother's dress is densely painted in broad black strokes. Agitated lines of paint reverberate around the figure of Jean and particularly around his tiny hand, suggesting that he is grasping at the dish. Bonnard has painted this scene quickly as he attempts to capture a likeness of the active infant. By contrast the 1895 picture has been executed with a greater emphasis on his personal artistic interests. The relative 'obedience' of his nephew, now a year older, enables him to infuse the scene with richer colours and to pay attention to the decorative patterns of the dish, Jean's shirt and the background wallpaper.

Bonnard is likely to have painted both scenes at Le Grand-Temps, his grandmother's home in the Dauphiné province where his extended family holidayed each summer.

36. Pierre Bonnard (1867-1947)

Boy eating Cherries, 1895

Oil on board, 52 x 41 cm

National Gallery of Ireland

37. Edouard Vuillard (1868-1940)

Two Seamstresses in the Workroom, 1893
Oil on mill board, 13.3 x 19.4 cm
Scottish National Gallery of Modern Art, Edinburgh.
Purchased with assistance from The Art Fund
and the National Heritage Memorial Fund 1990

In 1889 Vuillard joined The Nabis (*The Prophets*), a group of artists that also included Maurice Denis and Pierre Bonnard, and centred around Paul Sérusier. Inspired by the work of Paul Gauguin these artists painted from life. By reducing forms and simplifying colours, they aimed to convey the *essence* of their chosen subjects, that is to say, what they saw *and* how they experienced it.

Vuillard embraced these Nabis philosophies when he painted *Two Seamstresses in the Workroom*. Using bold impasto he flattened the three dimensional forms of the seamstresses to depict them with broad planes of exaggerated colour. Their overlapping dresses form a decorative blue screen against the yellow background.

The artist's home environment played a crucial role in the creation of his work, both in terms of subject matter and technique. Vuillard's mother ran a dressmaking business and he grew up with the familiar sight of seamstresses working in the family home. Here he not only depicts two seamstresses at work but also incorporates the materials they use into his composition. By reducing the women to semi-abstract forms with dots and daubs of pure pigment, Vuillard makes this small picture look like a colourful swatch of fabric.

38. Edouard Vuillard (1868-1940)

Interior, Mother and Sister of the Artist, 1893

Oil on canvas, 46.3 x 56.5 cm

The Museum of Modern Art, New York.

Gift of Mrs Saidie A. May, 1934

Vuillard is often quoted as having said 'I don't paint portraits. I paint people in their homes.'[1] In this dining room interior the Vuillard family home seems to assert a discomforting presence over the sitters, the artist's mother and his sister Marie.

Mme Vuillard sits just off centre in the composition. A solid figure in black, she strikes an authoritative, almost manly, pose. Resting her hands on open knees she looks directly out of the picture. Marie, by contrast, bends downwards as if compressed into a narrow space. She shrinks against the wall and presses her palms onto its densely patterned wallpaper. Whereas Mme Vuillard stands out against the room's yellow-brown background, Marie's hair and dress merge with the wallpaper. It is as if Marie crouches to keep 'out of frame' while the artist takes a 'snapshot' of her posing mother.

By cropping pictorial elements and distorting the compositional space, Vuillard undermines our expectations of balance. The furnishings and figures rest on floorboards that tilt forward sharply, like a raked stage. Nothing but the figure of Mme Vuillard seems to fit into place. It has been suggested that tensions between the two women may have influenced Vuillard's claustrophobic arrangement of the scene. In 1893 Marie married the artist Ker Xavier Roussel and her pose may reflect a desire to escape the strong presence of her mother. Perhaps it was because she married at the relatively late age of thirty-two that Vuillard depicted her as a 'wallflower'.

Vuillard was keenly involved in theatre design in the early 1890s. His familiarity with the plays of contemporaries such as Maurice Maeterlinck, Henrik Ibsen and August Strindberg undoubtedly informed the staging of this unsettling domestic scene.[2]

1 Quoted in Chastel 1946, p. 94.
2 Guy Cogeval and Antoine Salomon 2003, no IV. 112.

39. Edouard Vuillard (1868-1940)

The Manicure, 1897
Oil on board, 33.5 x 30 cm
Southampton City Art Gallery

Small in scale and intimate in setting, this painting exemplifies Vuillard's *intimisme*. A woman with a white cloth draped over her shoulder manicures the nails of a man seated with his back to the viewer. The scene is set in Thadée and Misia Natanson's apartment on the rue Saint-Florentin, identifiable by its stylised yellow and green wallpaper. Natanson was co-editor of the literary and artistic journal *La Revue Blanche*. His wife was an accomplished pianist, a celebrated beauty and host to artistic and literary gatherings. She counted Vuillard as one of her many male admirers and she sat for him in her apartment on many occasions.

Misia is the manicurist in this picture, her hair swept up in a characteristic topknot. The seated man is most likely the couple's friend, the writer Romain Coolus.[1] The ghostlike figure of Thadée Natanson stands at the right of the composition. As he witnesses the mundane, yet intimate, toilette ritual enacted by his wife and friend, his body seems to disintegrate and dissolve into the wallpaper. He is barely perceptible within the picture. Even the seated couple seem oblivious to his presence. Perhaps Vuillard's picture hints at Thadée's ineffectuality in preventing Misia's numerous love affairs.[2]

While Vuillard has purposely left the figurative elements of the picture indistinct he has, by contrast, paid great attention to its decorative detailing. Misia's red dress and Coolus's upholstered chair connect, creating a comfortable enclosure, from which the fading Thadée is excluded.

[1] Misia Natanson sits on this seat before the yellow wallpaper in *Woman seated on a Chair* (1896, Private Collection. A Vuillard photograph of Misia and Romain Coolus in the Natanson's apartment shows Coolus on a similar seat (1898, Private Collection), Cogeval 2003, cat. 177, p. 250.

[2] Both Coolus and Vuillard had relationships with Misia Natanson. See Guy Cogeval 2003, pp. 25-27

40. Edouard Vuillard (1868-1940)
Misia at Villeneuve-sur-Yonne, 1897-1899
Oil on canvas, 42.5 x 62.5 cm
Musée des Beaux Arts de Lyon

In the spring of 1897 Vuillard's friends Thadée and Misia Natanson bought Les Relais, a large country house at Villeneuve-sur-Yonne. There, Misia delighted in entertaining friends from artistic and literary circles, including Pierre Bonnard, Henri de Toulouse-Lautrec and Félix Vallottan. A regular visitor to the house, Vuillard painted many scenes showing friends eating, reading and relaxing in its gardens.

In this uncharacteristically minimalist composition, the artist shows Misia in the interior of the house, away from the lively groups that more typically populate his *Villeneuve-sur-Yonne* scenes. Framed by a doorway, she stands looking into the salon of Les Relais, which by comparison with her Parisian apartment (see cat. 39), is decorated in a simple, rustic fashion. The wastepaper bin and letter rack suggest the functionality of the room and the vernacular furniture indicates a fashionable interest in arts and crafts. The dotted blue pattern of Misia's dress is repeated on the foreground seat and on the surfaces of the table and shelf. This use of colour not only provides visual continuity but also highlights Misia's 'ownership' of the space. She fits into the recess of the doorway like an ornament in an alcove, the enigmatic focus of the room.

Vuillard has painted the walls in a dense impasto, which gives the room a rustic 'whitewashed' appearance. Areas of the canvas have been left unpainted, allowing its textured brown weave to emphasis elements of the composition, such as the edges of the table, the stacked letters and framing grey beams.

41. Edouard Vuillard (1868-1940)

Le Déjeuner, 1890s

Oil on canvas, 20 x 45 cm

Ashmolean Museum, Oxford

This work is one of many informal studies that Vuillard made of his mother in the cosy Montmartre apartment they shared with his sister Marie. Mme Vuillard sits at a dining table looking towards the viewer. Although the painting is entitled *Le Dejeuner*, no food appears to be laid on the table. Instead, the artist's mother reaches for a folded copy of a copy of a newspaper, *Le Figaro*, which takes a prominent position on the tablecoth. Mme Vuillard ran a corsetry and dressmaking business from the family home and is said to have used the dining room table as her office. She is frequently depicted reading newspapers in her son's pictures (cat. 43)

The dresser in the background indicates that the composition is set near a corner of the dining room and its shelves create an illusion of pictorial depth. Simultaneously and by contrast, the red expanses of the wall and Mme Vuillard's sprig-patterned dress serve to reduce the compositional space through their simple shapes. The painting's flattened space and matt surface create a decorative, collage-like appearance. Mme Vuillard's features are delineated by shadowy grey patches and stripes. This gives her face a mask-like quality that reflects her son's interests in theatre and Japanese art.

The heightened colouring, simplified forms and sections of dense patterning within this domestic interior are informed by Vuillard's involvement with Nabis group.

42. Edouard Vuillard (1868-1940)

Madame Vuillard arranging her Hair, 1900

Oil on millboard, 49.5 x 35.5 cm

The Trustees of the Barber Institute of Fine Arts,

University of Birmingham

In this painting Vuillard depicts his mother sitting in front of a mirror arranging her hair. The artist, who never married, lived with his mother until her death in 1928. Over a period of forty years, he depicted her everyday activities in hundreds of paintings and drawings. The composition is heavily patterned and the contrasting materials of Mme Vuillard's dress, the carpet and wallpaper compete for attention. These patterns are reflected back into the room by the mirror, heightening the claustrophobic effect. In this instance the artist's intimate subject matter, use of subdued colouring and inclusion of the mirror relate to his interest in seventeenth-century Dutch genre painting and in particular to the work of Johannes Vermeer.

Vuillard's creation of this 'snapshot' scene may have been aided by photographs, particularly as it would have been impossible for his elderly mother to hold this pose for a long time. Vuillard was a keen amateur photographer, and following the introduction of the portable Kodak camera in the mid 1890s, amassed a collection of over two thousand photographs, documenting his family, friends and home.

43. Edouard Vuillard (1868-1940)

The Fireplace, 1901

Oil on paper mounted on canvas, 46.2 x 62.2 cm

Saint Louis Art Museum, Funds given by Mr and Mrs John E. Simon

In this work Vuillard has edged the ever-present figure of his mother to the left-hand side of the composition, giving priority to the large central fireplace. Mme Vuillard sits with her legs stretched towards the heat emanating from the bright red fire. Reclining into her armchair, she reads a newspaper. As in *Interior, Mother and Sister of the Artist* (1893, cat. 38) Mme Vuillard's pose is comfortable and assured, perhaps even masculine. The mantelpiece displays a casually arranged clutter of bric-à-brac, ornaments and a potted cyclamen. Vuillard occasionally used mantelpiece surfaces as staging devices for his still-life compositions. In works such as *The Mantelpiece* (1905, Dublin City Gallery, The Hugh Lane Gallery) he created a display of contrasting patterns, surfaces and colours to great decorative effect.

Vuillard painted *The Fireplace* on brown paper and deliberately left patches unpainted to add a sense of warmth that is particularly appropriate to this cosy hearthside scene.

44. Edouard Vuillard (1868-1940)

The Hessels' Apartment, rue de Rivoli, 1903
Gouache on cardboard, 41 x 53.9 cm
National Gallery of Ireland

In 1900 Vuillard embarked on a close friendship with Lucy Hessel, the wife of Jos Hessel, his new art-dealer at the Bernheim-jeune Gallery. Their intimate relationship lasted until the artist's death some forty years later. It gave Vuillard's art a new impetus and Mme Hessel, like the artist's mother, assumed a muse-like role, featuring frequently in his interior scenes.

This sketch depicts Lucy in her dressing room in the Hessel's stylish apartment on the rue de Rivoli. She is seated with her back to the viewer in the presence of a man thought to be either her husband or the writer Romain Coolus. Although substantial in scale, this work is loosely executed in muted, rather muddied tones. It is one of several preliminary studies of the dressing room that informed Vuillard's painting *Interior at Night, the Hessels in their Dressing Room, rue de Rivoli* (1903, Private Collection).[1] Between 1900 and 1908, Vuillard visited the Hessel's apartment with such regularity that their servants came to call him the 'house painter'.

[1] Thomson 1991, p. 58.

45. Maurice Denis (1870-1943)

The Crown of Daisies, c.1905-1906

Oil on canvas, 73 x 54.5 cm

Carmen Thyssen-Bornemisza Collection

on loan to the Museo Thyssen-Bornemisza

While studying at the Académie Julian (1888-90) Maurice Denis joined Paul Sérusier, Paul Ranson and Pierre Bonnard in founding the Nabis. This group of artists looked to the work of Gauguin and Emile Bernard for inspiration. Rejecting the academic naturalism advocated by their teachers, Nabis painters aspired to convey a new type of artistic 'realism' by invoking subjective experiences. Their art involved the use of non-representative colouring and a movement towards decorative abstraction.

Denis, who was a devout Catholic, was deeply influenced by Italian Primitive art. In the 1890s he began to channel his Nabis interests in pure colour and patterning away from abstraction and into a deeply personal artistic style based on religious symbolism. Throughout his career his art was motivated by a desire to reinvent religious iconography and to transpose its motifs upon modern day subjects. The artist's family and home life strongly inspired his quasi-religious subjects and he repeatedly depicted his wife Marthe as a symbolic Madonna figure, attending to their numerous children.

Denis based the figures in *The Crown of Daisies* on Marthe and his daughter Bernadette (b.1899).[1] The figures of mother and child stand in an alcove in front of a wide open window. Beyond the window stretches an abstracted landscape, which may be based on Denis's home at Saint-Germain-en-Laye. On one level the painting can be simply understood as a genre-scene involving a girl making a daisy chain for her mother. Denis however, imbues the interaction between his 'madonna and child' with a symbolic weight, particularly through the use of stylised ceremonial gestures derived from Italian Primitive art: the bowing, the crowning and the 'plucking' hand movements.

Denis has painted this vibrant scene using broad patches, dots and daubs of pure colour. The dresses of the mother and child are conveyed in deep reds, oranges and coral pinks. The intimate inner space they occupy is similarly toned, which serves to separate them from the outside world and to heighten the joyful intensity of the moment.

1 Denis's *Maternity at the Window (Le Pouldou)*, (Musée d'Orsay, Paris) shows Marthe standing by an open window holding a baby, most likely the newborn Bernadette.

46. Pierre Bonnard (1867-1947)

Le Déjeuner, 1923
Oil on canvas, 41.3 x 62.2 cm
National Gallery of Ireland

Le Déjeuner is set the dining room of Bonnard's country house *Ma Roulotte* (*My Caravan*) at Vernonnet in the Seine valley. The artist bought the villa in 1912 and thereafter its sunny dining room and overgrown garden became favourite settings for his paintings. Bonnard would often paint mealtimes set against the dining room's wide open doors and windows to create the appearance of indoor 'picnics'. In this work the artist sits at a table with his companion Marthe de Méligny (who he married in 1925). The picture is designed both as an exercise in form and colour and as a celebration of the simple pleasures of everyday life. Bonnard creates a characteristically informal scene by using a 'snap-shot' arrangement of figures and objects. The dishes of fruit, crumpled napkin and half-empty bottle of wine, as well as the relaxed demeanour of the couple, suggest that the luncheon has ended. Marthe's red striped shirt featured in several of Bonnard's paintings between 1922 and 1928, where it introduced a clashing note of colour.

Central to the composition is the wide tabletop, which links the two figures. Tilted sharply and seen from a high view point it seems to nudge the man and woman towards the edges of the picture. Bonnard playfully uses the bold diagonal stripes of the tablecloth to distort perspective and enhance the decorative nature of the scene. The 'cut-off' elements of the painting relate to his interest in photography and Japanese art. It is very likely that Bonnard painted *Le Déjeuner* in his studio; working from sketches, photos and memory to create a composite of real and imagined detail. This motivation to paint from memory was intrinsically linked to his earlier Symbolist work and a desire to paint not just what was visible but what could be *felt*.

Although associated with Vuillard, Denis and Serusier in his early career, Bonnard developed an independent style that was constantly changing. He enjoyed renewed success in the 1920s, when this picture was painted, and his work was greatly admired by artists such as Matisse and Signac, who were similarly fascinated by colour and pattern. Bonnard painted landscapes, portraits and occasional cityscapes but throughout his long career was most deeply inspired by domestic interiors.

Selected Bibliography

Carol Armstrong, *Odd Man Out, Readings of the Work and Reputation of Edgar Degas* (Chicago and London 1991).

Christoph Asendorf, *Batteries of Life: On the history of things and their perception in modernity* (Berkeley 1993).

Leora Auslander, *Taste and Power: Furnishing Modern France* (Berkeley 1996).

Jeremy Aynsley and Charlotte Grant, eds, *Imagined Interiors: Representing the Domestic Interior since the Renaissance* (London 2006).

Colin B. Bailey, Linda Nochlin and Anne Distel, *Renoir's Portraits: Impressions of an Age*, exh. cat. National Gallery of Art, Ottawa and Kimbell Art Museum, Forth Worth (1997).

Judith A. Barter, 'Mary Cassatt: Themes, Sources, and the Modern Woman', in *Mary Cassatt: Modern Woman*, exh. cat. The Art Institute of Chicago (1998), pp. 45-107.

Charles Baudelaire, 'The Painter of Modern Life', in *The Painter of Modern Life and other Essays* (London and New York 1995), pp. 1-41.

Charles Baudelaire, *Œuvres complètes*, 2 vols (Paris 1975-76).

Felix Baumann and Marianne Karabelnik, eds, *Degas Portraits* (London 1994).

Christopher Benfey, *Degas in New Orleans: Encounters in the Creole World of Kate Chopin and George Washington Cable* (New York 1997).

Walter Benjamin, *The Arcades Project* (Cambridge, Mass. and London 1999).

Walter Benjamin, 'Paris, Capital of the Nineteenth-Century', in *Reflections, Essays, Aphorisms, Autobiographical Writings* (New York 1978), pp.146-62.

Francesca Berry, 'Lived Perspectives: The Art of the French Nineteenth-Century Interior', Jeremy Aynsley and Charlotte Grant, eds, *Imagined Interiors: Representing the Domestic Interior since the Renaissance* (London 2006), pp.160-83.

Ruth Berson, *The New Painting: Impressionism, 1874-1886. Documentation*, 2 vols (San Francisco 1996).

Andreas Bluhm and Louise Lippincott, *Light! The Industrial Age 1750-1900, Art & Science, Technology & Society*, exh. cat. Van Gogh Museum, Amsterdam and Carnegie Museum of Art, Pittsburgh (2000).

Jean Sutherland Boggs et al, *Degas*, exh. cat., Galeries Nationales du Grand Palais, Paris, The Metropolitan Museum of Art, New York and National Gallery of Canada, Ottawa (1988).

Jean Sutherland Boggs et al, *Degas at the Races*, exh. cat. National Gallery of Art, Washington DC (1998).

Suzanne Boorsch, 'Fireworks! Four Centuries of Pyrotechnics in Prints and Drawings', The Metropolitan Museum of Art Bulletin (Summer 2000).

Richard R. Brettell and Anne-Birgitte Fonsmark, *Gauguin and Impressionism*, exh. cat. Kimbell Art Museum and Ordupgaard, Copenhagen (2005).

Richard Brettell et al, *The Art of Paul Gauguin*, exh. cat. National Gallery of Art, Washington DC (1988).

Norma Broude, ed., *Gustave Caillebotte and the Fashioning of Identity in Impressionist Paris* (New Brunswick, New Jersey and London 2002).

Marilyn R. Brown, 'Degas and 'A Cotton Office in New Orleans', *The Burlington Magazine*, vol. 130, no. 1020 (March 1988), pp. 216-21.

Lillian Browse, *Degas Dancers* (London 1949).

Françoise Cachin, Charles S. Moffet and Juliet Wilson Bareau, *Manet, 1832-1883*, exh. cat. Galeries nationales du Grand Palais, Paris, and Metropolitan Museum of Art, New York (1983).

André Chastel, *Vuillard 1868-1940* (Paris 1946).

Petra ten-Doesschate Chu, ed, *Letters of Gustave Courbet* (Chicago, 1992).

Petra ten-Doesschate Chu, 'The Lu(c)re of London: French Artists and Art Dealers in the British Capital, 1859-1914', in *Monet's London: Artists' Reflections on the Thames, 1859-1914*, exh. cat. Museum of Fine Arts, St. Petersburg, Florida (2005), pp. 39-54

T. J. Clark, *The Painting of Modern Life. Paris in the Art of Manet and His Followers* (London 1984).

Hollis Clayson, 'Maternity as Alibi in Mary Cassatt's Paintings of Women and Children,' for web site of the Musée d'Art Américain, Giverny, France (2001). Available as unpublished paper.

Hollis Clayson, *Painted Love, Prostitution in French Art of the Impressionist Era* (New Haven and London 1991).

Hollis Clayson, *Paris in Despair: Art and Everyday Life under Siege (1870-1871)* (Chicago 2002).

Hollis Clayson, 'Looking within the Cell of Privacy', in Peter Parshall, ed., *The Darker Side of Light: The Arts of Privacy, 1850-1900* (forthcoming).

Guy Cogeval and Antoine Salomon, *Vuillard: Critical Catalogue of Paintings and Pastels* (Paris 2003).

Guy Cogeval, *Édouard Vuillard*, exh. cat. Montreal Museum of Fine Arts and National Gallery of Art, Washington, DC (2003).

James Cuno and Joachim Kaak, eds, *Manet Face to Face*, exh.cat. Courtauld Institute Galleries and Neue Pinakothek, Munich (2004).

Edgar Degas, *Letters* (Oxford 1947).

Anne Distel et al, *Gustave Caillebotte: Urban Impressionist*, exh. cat. La Réunion des Musées Nationaux, Musée d'Orsay, Paris and the Art Institute of Chicago (1995).

Therese Dolan, 'A Model Complicated by an Artist', in Sidsel Maria Søndergaard, ed., *Women in Impressionism, From Mythical Feminine to Modern Woman*, exh. cat. Ny Carlsberg Glyptotek, Copenhagen (Milan 2006), pp. 135-55.

Ann Dumas, Colta Ives, Susan Alyson Stein and Gary Tinterow, *The Private Collection of Edgar Degas*, exh. cat. The Metropolitan Museum of Art, New York (1998).

Ann Dumas, *Degas and the Italians in Paris*, exh. cat. National Galleries of Scotland, Edinburgh (2003).

Edmond Duranty, *La nouvelle peinture à propos du groupe d'artistes qui expose dans les galeries de Durand-Ruel* (Paris 1876).

Edmond Duranty, 'Sur la physionomie', *La Revue Libérale*, no. 2 (25 July 1867), pp. 499-523.

T. J. Edelstein, ed., *Perspectives on Morisot* (New York 1990).

Gail Feigenbaum et al, *Degas and New Orleans: a French Impressionist in America*, exh. cat. New Orleans Museum of Art and Ordrupgaard (Copenhagen 1999).

Priscilla Parkhurst Ferguson, 'The Flâneur: The City and Its Discontents', *Paris as Revolution: Writing the Nineteenth-Century City* (Berkeley 1994), pp. 80-114.

Marina Ferretti-Bocquillon et al., *Signac, 1863-1935*, exh. cat. The Metropolitan Museum of Art (2001).

Gustave Flaubert, *Correspondance*, vol. II (July 1851- December 1858), (Paris 1980).

Sharon Flescher, *Zacharie Astruc: Critic, Artist and Japoniste (1833-1907)* (New York 1977).

Penny Florence, *Mallarmé, Manet and Redon, Visual and Aural Signs and the Generation of Meaning* (Cambridge 1986).

Françoise Forster-Hahn et al., *Spirit of an Age: Nineteenth-Century Paintings from the Nationalgalerie, Berlin*, exh. cat. National Gallery, London (2001).

Adrian Forty, *Objects of Desire: Design and Society from Wedgewood to IBM* (New York 1986).

Bruno Foucart, 'Histoire de l'art et histoire de l'électricité: L'histoire de l'art face à l'électricité' in Fabienne Cardot, ed., *L'électricité dans l'histoire: problèmes et méthodes* (Paris 1985), pp. 147-54.

Michael Fried, *Manet's Modernism, or, the Face of Painting in the 1860s* (Chicago 1996).

Diana Fuss, *The Sense of an Interior: Four Writers and the Rooms that Shaped Them* (New York and London 2004).

Lynn Garafola, 'The Travesty Dancer in Nineteenth-Century Ballet', Lesley Ferris, ed., *Crossing the Stage: controversies on cross-dressing* (London 1993), pp. 96-106.

Mark Girouard, *The Victorian Country House* (New Haven and London 1979).

John Gloag, *Victorian comfort: a social history of design from 1830-1900* (Newton Abbot 1973).

Edmond de Goncourt, *La Maison d'un artiste*, vol. I (Dijon 2003).

Jean-Christophe Gourvennec, ed., *Henri Gervex, 1852-1929*, exh. cat. Galerie des Beaux-Arts, Bordeaux (1992).

Gloria Groom, *Gustave Caillebotte: Urban Impressionist* (Paris and Chicago 1995).

June Hargrove, 'Modern Melancholy: Degas's portrait of Duranty in his study', in Leïla El-Wakil, Stéphanie Pallini and Lada Umstätter-Mamedova, eds, *Études transversals, mélanges en l'honneur de Pierre Vaisse* (Lyon 2005), pp. 171-78.

Charles Harrison, Paul Wood and Jason Gaiger, eds, *Art in Theory, 1815-1900: an anthology of changing ideas* (Oxford 1998).

David Harvey, *Consciousness and the Urban Experience: studies in the history and theory of capitalist urbanisation* (Baltimore 1985).

Louisine W. Havemeyer, *Sixteen to Sixty: Memoirs of a Collector* (New York, 1961).

F.W.J. Hemmings et Robert J. Niess, eds, *Émile Zola. Salons.* (Geneva and Paris 1959).

Hilde Heynen and Gülsüm Baydar, eds, *Negotiating Domesticity: spatial productions of gender in modern architecture* (London 2005).

Anne Higonnet, *Berthe Morisot's Images of Women* (Cambridge, Mass. and London 1992).

John House, *Impressionism: Paint and Politics* (New Haven and London 2004).

John House, *Impressionists by the Sea*, exh. cat. Royal Academy of Arts, London (2007).

John House, 'New Material on Monet and Pissarro in London in 1870-71,' *The Burlington Magazine*, vol. 120, no. 907 (October 1978), pp. 636-42.

J.K. Huysmans, *L'Art moderne* (Paris 1883).

J.K. Huysmans, *Parisian Sketches* (Sawtry 2004).

Ruth E. Iskin, *Modern Women and Parisian Consumer Culture in Impressionist Painting* (Cambridge 2007).

Richard Kendall, *Degas Backstage* (London 1996).

Richard Kendall, *Degas by Himself* (London 2004).

Richard Kendall, ed., *Degas. Images of Women*, exh. cat., Tate Gallery Liverpool (1989).

Richard Kendall and Griselda Pollock, eds, *Dealing with Degas: Representations of Women and the Politics of Vision* (London 1992).

Pat Kirkham, ed., *The Gendered Object* (Manchester 1996).

Pierre Larousse, *Grand dictionnaire universel du XIXe siècle, français, historique, géographique, mythologique, bibliographique, littéraire, artistique, scientifique*, 17 vols (Paris 1864-1890).

Thomas Lederballe and Rebecca Rabinow, eds, *The Age of Impressionism: European Painting from the Ordrupgaard Collection, Copenhagen*, exh. cat. Ordrupgaard, Copenhagen (2002).

Anne Leonard, 'Picturing Listening in the Late Nineteenth Century', *The Art Bulletin* vol. LXXXIX, no. 2 (June 2007), pp. 266-86.

Mary Tompkins Lewis, ed., *Critical readings in Impressionism and post-Impressionism: An Anthology* (Berkeley and London 2007).

Nancy Locke, *Manet and the Family Romance* (Princeton and Oxford 2001).

François Loyer, *Paris-Nineteenth Century: architecture and urbanism* (New York 1988).

Henri Loyrette, *Degas inédit: actes du colloque Degas* (Paris 1989)

Kenneth McConkey, *Impressionism in Britain* (New Haven and London 1995).

Michael McKeon, *The Secret History of Domesticity: public, private, and the division of knowledge* (Baltimore and London 2005).

Didier Maleuvre, *Museum Memories: history, technology, art* (Stanford 1999).

Stéphane Mallarmé, 'The Impressionists and Edouard Manet', *The Art Monthly Review*, vol. I (30 September 1876), pp. 117-22.

Sharon Marcus, *Apartment Stories: city and home in nineteenth-century Paris and London* (Berkeley and London 1999).

Nancy Rose Marshall and Malcolm Warner, *James Tissot: Victorian Life / Modern Love* (Yale and London 1999).

Nancy Mowll Mathews and Barbara Stern Shapiro, *Mary Cassatt: the color prints* (New York and Williamstown, Mass. 1989).

Charles S. Moffett et al, *The New Painting: Impressionism 1874-1886*, exh. cat. Fine Arts Museums of San Francisco (1986).

George Moore, *Confessions of a Young Man* (London 1952).

Berthe Morisot, *The correspondence of Berthe Morisot with her family and her friends Manet, Puvis de Chavannes, Degas, Monet, Renoir and Mallarmé* (London, 1986).

Linda Nochlin, *The Politics of Vision: Essays on Nineteenth-Century Art and Society* (London, 1991).

Donald J. Olsen, *The City as a Work of Art: London, Paris, Vienna* (New Haven and London 1986).

Rozsika Parker and Griselda Pollock, *Old Mistresses: women, art and ideology* (London 1981).

Michelle Perrot, ed., *A History of Private Life. Volume 4: From the Fires of Revolution to the Great War* (Cambridge, Mass and London 1990).

David Pinkney, *Napoleon III and the Rebuilding of Paris* (Princeton 1958).

Joachim Pissarro, *Pissarro: Critical Catalogue of Paintings* (London 2005)

Griselda Pollock, *Mary Cassatt: painter of modern women* (London 1998).

Griselda Pollock, *Vision and Difference: femininity, feminism and the history of art* (London and New York 1988).

Marla Prather and Charles F. Stuckey, eds, *Gauguin. A Retrospective* (New York 1987).

Christopher Reed, ed., *Not at Home: the suppression of domesticity in modern art and architecture* (London 1996).

Sue Welsh Reed and Barbara Stern Shapiro, *Edgar Degas: the painter as printmaker* (Boston 1984).

Theodore Reff, 'Degas's "Tableau de Genre"', *The Art Bulletin*, vol. 54, no. 3 (September 1972), pp. 316-37.

Theodore Reff, *Degas. The Artist's Mind* (New York 1976).

John Rewald, *Studies in Impressionism* (London 1985).

Charles Rice, *The Emergence of the Interior: architecture, modernity, domesticity* (London 2007).

Victoria Rosner, *Modernism and the Architecture of Private Life* (New York 2005).

Witold Rybczynski, *Home. A Short History of an Idea* (New York 1986).

Remy Saisselin, *Bricabracomania. The Bourgeois and the Bibelot* (London 1985).

Wolfgang Schivelbusch, *Disenchanted Night. The Industrialization of Light in the Nineteenth Century* (Berkeley and London 1988).

Wolfgang Schivelbusch, 'Panoramic Travel', in Vanessa R. Schwartz and Jeannene M. Przyblyski, eds, *The Nineteenth-Century Visual Culture Reader* (New York 2004), pp. 92-99.

Richard Sennett, *The Fall of Public Man*, (New York 1978).

Michael Edward Shapiro, 'Degas and the Siamese Twins of the Café Concert: The Ambassadors and the Alcazar d'Été', *Gazette des Beaux-Arts* (April 1980), pp. 153-64.

Jennifer Shaw, 'The Figure of Venus: rhetoric of the ideal and the Salon of 1863', *Art History* vol. 14, no.4 (December 1991), pp. 540-63.

Richard Shiff, *Cézanne and the End of Impressionism. A Study of the Theory, Technique, and Critical Evaluation of Modern Art* (Chicago and London 1984).

Susan Sidlauskas, *Body, Place, and Self in Nineteenth-Century Painting* (Cambridge and New York 2000).

Susan Sidlauskus, 'Resisting Narrative: the problem of Edgar Degas's *Interior*', *Art Bulletin*, no.75 (December 1993), pp. 671-96.

Debora Silverman, *Art Nouveau in fin de siècle France: politics, psychology, and style* (Berkeley and London 1989).

Debora Silverman, 'A Fin de Siècle Interior and the Psyche. The Soul Box of Dr. Jean-Martin Charcot', *Daidalos*, no. 28, 15 June 1988, pp. 24-31.

Robert Snell, *Théophile Gautier, A Romantic Critic of the Visual Arts* (Oxford 1982).

Judith F. Stone, 'The Republican Brotherhood: Gender and Ideology', in Elinor Accampo, Rachel Fuchs, and Mary Lynn Stewart, eds, *Gender and the Politics of Social Reform in France, 1870-1914* (Baltimore 1995), pp. 28-58.

Anthony Sutcliffe, *Paris. An Architectural History* (New Haven and London 1993).

Keith Tester, ed., *The Flâneur* (London and New York 1994).

Belinda Thomson, *Vuillard: a national touring exhibition from the South Bank Centre*, exh. cat. South Bank Centre, London (1991).

Richard Thomson, *Edgar Degas. Waiting* (Malibu 1995).

Théophile Thoré (William Bürger), 'Van der Meer de Delft', *Gazette des Beaux Arts*, 21 (October-December 1866), pp. 297-330, 458-470, 542-575.

Pamela Todd, *The Impressionists at Home* (London 2005).

Kirk Varnedoe, *Gustave Caillebotte* (New Haven and London 1987).

Eugène Emmanuel Viollet-le-Duc, *Lectures on Architecture*, vol. 2 (New York 1987).

H. Barbara Weinberg et al, *Childe Hassam: American Impressionist*, exh. cat. Metropolitan Museum of Art, New York (2004).

Jeff Weintraub and Krishan Kumar, eds, *Public and Private in Thought and Practice: perspectives on a grand dichotomy* (Chicago and London 1997).

Michael Wentworth, *James Tissot* (Oxford 1984).

Edmund White, *The Flâneur. A Stroll through the Paradoxes of Paris* (London 2001).

Juliet Wilson-Bareau, ed., *Manet by himself: correspondence and conversation, paintings, pastels, prints and drawings* (London 2004).

Juliet Wilson-Bareau and David Degener, *Manet and the Sea*, exh. cat. Art Institute of Chicago, Philadelphia Museum of Art and Van Gogh Museum, Amsterdam (2003).

Janet Wolff, *Feminine Sentences: essays on women and culture* (Berkeley 1990).

Photo credits

© ADAGP, Paris and DACS, London 2008. Ashmolean Museum, University of Oxford: cat. 41

© ADAGP, Paris and DACS, London 2008. Courtesy of The Barber Institute of Fine Arts, University of Birmingham: cat. 42

© ADAGP, Paris and DACS, London 2008. Courtesy of the Saint Louis Art Museum, Funds given by Mr and Mrs John E. Simon: cat. 43

© ADAGP, Paris and DACS, London 2008. Courtesy of the Scottish National Gallery of Modern Art. Purchased with assistance from The Art Fund (Scottish Fund) and the National Heritage Memorial Fund 1990: cat. 37

© ADAGP, Paris and DACS, London 2008. Image © 2008, The Museum of Modern Art, New York / Scala, Florence: cat. 38

© ADAGP, Paris and DACS, London 2008. Musée des Beaux Arts de Lyon. Photo © MBA Lyon / Alain Basset: cat. 40

© ADAGP, Paris and DACS, London, 2008. Photo © Leeds Museums and Galleries (City Art Gallery) UK / The Bridgeman Art Library: cat. 35

© ADAGP, Paris and DACS, London 2008. Photo © National Gallery of Ireland: cats. 36, 44, 46

© ADAGP, Paris and DACS, London 2008. Photo © Southampton City Art Gallery, Hampshire, UK. The Bridgeman Art Library: cat. 39

Bequest of Louise Taft Semple, Taft Museum of Art, Cincinnati, Ohio. Photographer: Tony Walsh: Singletary fig. 3

Bibliothèque Nationale de France: Singletary fig. 1

bpk/Nationalgalerie, SMB/ Jorg P. Anders: cat. 14

Collection Carmen Thyssen-Bornemisza on loan to the Museo Thyssen-Bornemisza: cat. 28

Collection of the Flint Institute of Arts, Flint, Michigan: cat. 20

Collection Mondadori, Museo Civico di Palazzo Te Mantova: cat. 27

Courtesy of the Corcoran Gallery of Art, Washington, DC, Museum Purchase, Gallery Fund: Clayson fig. 4

Courtesy of the Musée d'Orsay, Paris. Photo © RMN / Gerard Blot: Clayson fig. 2, Singletary fig. 7

Courtesy of the Museum of Fine Arts, Boston, Gift of William Emerson and The Hayden Collection - Charles Henry Hayden Fund: Clayson fig. 10

Courtesy of the Wadsworth Atheneum Museum of Art, Hartford, CT. The Ella Gallup Sumner and Mary Catlin Sumner Collection Fund: cat. 15

© DACS, 2008. Photo© VEGAP, 2008. Carmen Thyssen-Bornemisza Collection on loan to the Museo Thyssen-Bornemisza: cat. 45

Image Courtesy of the Board of Trustees, National Gallery of Art, Washington: Clayson fig. 1, comparative image p. 58, cats. 17, 21

Image courtesy of the Board of Trustees, National Gallery of Art, Washington, Rosenwald Collection: Clayson fig. 8

Image © The Metropolitan Museum of Art: cat. 12, detail p. 30

J. P. Godais. Cliché ville d'Evreux. Musee d'Evreux: cat. 13

Kitakyushu Municipal Museum of Art: Singletary fig. 4

Kunsthalle Bremen-Der Kunstverein in Bremen. Photographer: Lars Lohrisch: Singletary fig. 10

Musée des Beaux-Arts de Lyon. © MBA Lyon / Alain Basset: cat. 4

Musée Marmottan Monet, Paris, France/The Bridgeman Art Library: cat. 23

Nasjonalmuseet, Oslo. Photo: J. Lathion © Nasjonalmuseet 2008: detail p. 3, Singletary fig. 5, cat. 19

Ny Carlsberg Glyptotek, Copenhagen. Photographer Ole Haupt: cat. 33